GREAT ESCAPES
OF WORLD WAR II

GREAT ESCAPES OF WORLD WAR II

George Sullivan

SCHOLASTIC INC.
New York Toronto London Auckland Sydney

ISBN 0-590-43800-X

12 11 10 9 8 7 6   2/0

Printed in the U.S.A.   01

Contents

Acknowledgments

The author is grateful to the following publishers for permission to include material from the sources mentioned in this book:

Random House, Inc., for selected excerpts from *The Faustball Tunnel* by John Hammond Moore, © 1978 by John Hammond Moore.

Henry Holt, Inc., for a specified condensation from *Ten Escape From Tojo* by Commander Melvyn H. McCoy and Lieutenant S. M. Melnik, © 1944 by Farrar and Rinehart, and renewed in 1972 by Holt, Rinehart and Winston, Inc.

Bergin & Garvey Publishers, Inc., for selected excerpts from *Escape From Auschwitz* by Erich Kulka, © 1986 by Bergin & Garvey Publishers, Inc.

For selected excerpts reprinted from *The Great Escape* by Paul Brickhill, by permis-

Introduction

World War II, the biggest, most destructive war in history, produced more prisoners than any other war. In much of Europe and in Japan and southeast Asia, hundreds of thousands of prisoners from the United States, Canada, Great Britain, and other Allied nations were kept captive.

There were also prisoners from Germany, Italy, and Japan held in the United States. At one time, the number was close to half a million.

A prisoner of war is defined as any captured member of a warring country's armed forces. Prisoners of war are often called P.O.W.'s.

In most cases, prisoners were individuals who surrendered to the enemy. Sometimes, however, they had been taken by force.

Nations of the world have tried to provide for the fair treatment of prisoners of war. The Hague Conventions of 1899 and 1907 and the Geneva Convention of 1929 established certain rules concerning the treatment of prisoners.

Those who had been captured did not have to give the enemy any information except their name, rank, and military serial number. Prisoners were permitted to send and receive mail.

Another regulation provided that representatives of nonwarring countries be permitted to inspect prison camps. In the case of the United States and other Allied nations, these inspections were often carried out by the International Committee of the Red Cross.

The inspections were meant to determine whether the prisons were safe and clean. They also were to make certain that prisoners were receiving enough food and proper medical care.

Nearly all the nations of the world agreed to follow the rules concerning prisoners of war that were fixed by the Hague and Geneva Conventions. Nevertheless, countless prisoners were treated harshly during World War II. Japan, Germany, and the Soviet Union came to be known for their brutal treatment of prisoners. Millions of them died as a result of cold, starvation, or plain mistreatment.

But most of the nations that took part in World War II respected prisoner-of-war regulations. The great majority of those taken prisoner survived the experience and were returned home after the war ended.

But being a prisoner of war was tough. Prisoners knew that they would remain captive for as long as the war lasted. But how long was it going to last? No one knew.

And there was the physical suffering — bad food, never having any privacy, and sometimes, rough treatment.

Escape was the only solution.

It's not hard to understand why some wartime prisoners chose not to wait until peace was declared to regain their freedom. Often displaying great courage and stamina, they managed to overcome the armed guards, iron bars, and barbed wire that held them. This book tells the story of some of these brave people.

Colditz

With its high granite walls, steep tile roofs, ancient towers, and barred windows, Colditz Castle looked like it belonged in a story about Dr. Frankenstein or Dracula. But a closer look revealed several modern touches. The castle's walls bristled with barbed wire and machine guns. Sentries were posted on the roofs.

Colditz Castle was one of the most notorious of all World War II prisons.

Located in eastern Germany, less than fifty miles from the Czechoslovakian border, Colditz had been built in the year 1014, almost five centuries before Columbus set out for the Americas. At the time, it served as a royal hunting lodge for the kings of Saxony.

Colditz became a prison in 1800, its living spaces converted into bare cells and dark dungeons. It first served as a prisoner-of-war camp in World War II after German forces had stormed through Poland in the fall of 1939. Polish prisoners were later joined by those from Belgium, France, the Netherlands, and Great Britain.

Early in the war, the German Army High Command decided Colditz would be special. It would be used to house prisoners who had made escape attempts in other prisons.

It seemed to make good sense to put all failed escapers under one roof, then tighten security so as to make it impossible for them to get out. But in practice, this wasn't the case. The castle presented a great challenge to the men held captive there. They considered it almost a duty to try to outwit the guards and security system. "Every man in this castle," a British officer once said, "has but one single thought — to escape."

The prisoners were amazingly inventive in their manufacture of tools and equipment to be used in escape attempts. German officers' uniforms were tailored from the prisoners' own uniforms. They were dyed the right color with a substance made from the ground-down lead obtained from colored pencils. Another source of dye was colored paper. From melted-down phonograph records poured into clay molds, they made buttons for uniforms and civilian clothing.

Floorboards provided the wood for skillfully carved imitation rifles. The necessary stamps for fake passports and identification papers were carved out of linoleum. Keys for the prison's locks were cut out of bucket handles, then filed to fit.

At the time of its peak use, Colditz held about 800 prisoners. Those involved in plotting escapes were able to make use of the prison's huge attic spaces, unused cellars, and countless empty rooms to work on their plans in secret.

About 130 Colditz prisoners were successful in getting outside the castle walls. Lt. Alain le Ray, a French officer, was the first. On April 11, 1941, le Ray was one of a group of prisoners being marched back to the prison after an exercise period in a park close to the castle. As the column of marchers rounded a curve, which obscured le Ray from the guards, he leaped down an embankment and hid himself in the cellar of a nearby house. The guards saw nothing and heard nothing.

Le Ray remained hidden for half an hour, then made his way safely through the park and over the low stone wall that surrounded it. He eventually found freedom in Switzerland.

In the years that followed, countless other types of escapes were attempted. Some groups of prisoners tried wriggling their way through Colditz's dank, brick-lined sewers. Others tried to tunnel their way out, spending month after month scraping and digging, moving tons of earth and rock.

There were prisoners who made bedsheet ropes and tried dropping out of windows. Prisoners sought to conceal themselves in mailbags, hoping that the Germans would simply truck them through the prison gates.

Virtually all of the escape tries involved months of careful planning and preparation. One such attempt was the brainchild of Capt. Machiel van den Heuvel, a Dutch officer.

For several months, van den Heuvel observed the routine followed each week by four Polish prisoners. Their job was to collect the soiled uniforms of German officers from a storeroom outside the castle's north wall. After they had loaded the clothing into two big wooden crates, the Poles picked up the crates by their rope handles and were escorted by a pair of

German guards a quarter of a mile from the castle. There, the Poles washed and ironed the uniforms.

Van den Heuvel's plan was to choose six men to impersonate the four Polish laundry workers and their two guards, then duplicate what they had been doing — filling the wooden crates with dirty clothes and carrying them through the security gate to the laundry. That would put the six men within easy walking distance of the park — and freedom.

The first problem was to get into the storeroom where the dirty uniforms were collected. Pat Reid, a British prisoner who had been let in on the plan, noticed that the storeroom was directly underneath an office. Reid believed it would be possible to gain entry to the storeroom by going through the floor of the office.

The office belonged to a German sergeant named Feldwebel Gephard, who was in charge of the laundry workers. It happened that Gephard's office was located just across the corridor from a large room that served as a sick ward for prisoners.

Capt. Kenneth Lockwood, another British prisoner, was able to get himself admitted to the ward by faking stomach cramps. Late one afternoon, Reid and Derek Gill, yet another British prisoner, paid a visit to their "sick" friend to cheer him up. When the hospital guards were not looking, Reid and Gill hid themselves under Lockwood's bed.

Not long after, visiting hours ended and the ward was locked for the night. Reid and Gill then reappeared from under the bed. Lockwood had been provided with duplicate keys, and with these he unlocked the ward doors and the door to Gephard's office. It was a simple matter to let Reid and Gill into the office, relock the door, and return to his hospital bed.

Once inside the office, Reid and Gill knew exactly what to do. They first removed enough floorboards to expose the mortar of the storeroom ceiling. The two men worked through the night, scraping away the mortar that had deteriorated badly through the years and offered little resistance.

At the first light of dawn, Reid and Gill stopped work and began replacing the floorboards. Everything had to look exactly as they had found it. Even the floorboard nails were put back in their original holes. Reid had brought along a container of dust that the two men used to fill the gaps between the boards.

They were waiting when Lockwood unlocked the office door. They crossed the corridor to the hospital ward and again hid themselves under Lockwood's bed. They were later able to slip out of the ward and return to their quarters in time for morning roll call.

The next night the scene was replayed. Reid and Gill were able to make the hole in the floor big enough so that they could fit through it. All they now had to do was break through the thin layer left in the ceiling below them to gain entry to the storeroom.

Meanwhile, other prisoners had set to work making the uniforms to be worn by the six men who would be attempting the escape — the four uniforms of the Polish laundry workers and the two uniforms of the German guards.

Once outside the prison walls, the plan called for the six men to assume identities of Dutch civilian workers. They also had to be provided with civilian clothing, and a prison forger began preparing identification papers for each man.

Prisoners who were skilled as carpenters began to make the wooden crates that were to serve as containers for the laundry. The crates had to look exactly like the originals, complete with rope handles.

The day set for the escape attempt finally arrived. It was decided to make the attempt at 7 o'clock in the morning. That's when one set of security guards was relieved by another. The men who planned the escape were confident that the guards coming on duty would take it for granted that the laundry workers and their guards had entered the storeroom before their tour of duty had begun.

The night before, the wooden boxes, divided into several sections, were smuggled into the hospital ward and hidden under beds. By now, the men who were to attempt the escape had been chosen. Three of the men were Dutch: Herman Donkers, Damiaan van Doorninck, and Ted Beets; and three were British: Bill Lawton, Hank Wardle, and Bill Fowler.

On the night before the escape, the six men began arriving at the hospital ward one by one. Lockwood opened Gephard's office and admitted each man. Reid and Gill showed up, too, to help out.

By 10 P.M., all the members of the escape party were inside Gephard's office. Lockwood secured the door's padlock and returned to his ward bed. The drop into the storeroom was planned for 2 o'clock the next morning.

Time passed slowly as the men waited. Some dozed. Those too excited to nap spoke in muffled tones. Suddenly the stillness was shattered by the loud clang of the prison alarm. The men knew at once what that meant. Their quarters had been searched and the absence of one or more of them had been discovered.

Sickening fear swept over the men. They knew that if they tried to go back they would be discovered. It was much too early to go forward. All they could do was remain as silent as possible.

They heard the German patrols setting out to search the castle. One entered the building in which they were hiding. Their hearts pounded as they heard the stamp of approaching boots. The patrol stopped just outside Gephard's door. An officer spoke: "This door is padlocked. There's no one in there. Let's move on." The men inside Gephard's office could hardly believe their good luck.

After the patrol had left, the remaining time passed quietly. At 2 A.M., the men stirred and watched anxiously as Reid and Gill began removing the floorboard nails. Then they pried the boards free. Reid wriggled into the hole and broke through the ceiling of the storeroom.

One by one, the men dropped feetfirst through the hole into the storeroom. Van Doorninck went first, followed by Lawton and the others. Reid and Gill were to remain behind to replace the floorboards. They hoped to be able to prevent the Germans from finding out about the escape route. Perhaps other prisoners could make use of it.

Gill had brought along a small bag of plaster and a container of water. The plaster was to be used to seal the hole in the storeroom ceiling.

Reid and Gill handed through the German uniforms that the "guards" were to wear to the men in the storeroom. The other clothing and the sections of wood that would go to form the two crates were passed through, too.

Once safely in the storeroom, van Doorninck put on a German sergeant's uniform, and Donkers, a German private's. The four other men changed into their laundry-worker uniforms.

As the men assembled the boxes, van Doorninck plastered the hole in the ceiling. On the other side, Reid and Gill had already replaced the floorboards and left Gephard's office.

Shortly after 7 A.M., the men were ready to make their bold attempt. Lawton and Fowler grasped the rope handles of one crate, and Wardle and Beets, the handles of the other. "Sergeant" van Doorninck opened the storeroom door and led the escape party out into the pale early-morning sunlight.

Van Doorninck went first, then Wardle and Beets with their crate between them, then Lawton and Fowler, with "Private" Donkers bringing up the rear.

The party walked confidently past the first sentry, who hardly glanced at them. Fifty yards beyond, another sentry was posted. He paid no attention to them, either.

Van Doorninck and the others knew that the real test would come at the castle security gate. Van Doorninck had no key to the gate. His plan was to order the sentry to open it.

As they approached the gate, the sentry looked up. "Are you going to the laundry?" he asked van Doorninck.

The Dutch officer answered yes in his very best German. The sentry graciously unlocked the gate and swung it open. The six men marched through.

As they continued walking, they heard the gate slam shut behind them. They had done it. They had escaped from Colditz by walking out right under the noses of the German guards.

The men were now in a park that was encircled by a low stone wall. They ducked into a wooded area of the park and there discarded the wooden crates and changed into the Dutch civilian clothes.

Donkers teamed up with Wardle, van Doorninck with Fowler, and Beets with Lawton. They went over the stone wall in pairs and fled through the countryside, each pair following a different route to Switzerland, some 300 miles to the south and west.

When roll call was held at the castle that morning, and all six men were discovered missing, the Germans assumed that they had escaped. They immediately launched a vigorous search of the surrounding area.

Lawton and Beets were recaptured that evening. Donkers and Wardle did a little better. They were spotted the next day at a railroad station a good distance from Colditz.

But van Doorninck and Fowler made it. On September 15, 1942, six days after they marched out of Colditz, they crossed the border into Switzerland.

On a sunny morning in April 1945, American troops, sweeping out of the west, stormed into the town of Colditz. They quickly liberated the 300 or so prisoners the castle held at the time, thus bringing to a close a frightful chapter in the thousand-year history of the castle.

In a matter of weeks, Germany surrendered to the Allies, ending the war in Europe. Colditz was not forgotten, for the stories of Allied prisoners and their daring escapes began to be told, and they are still being heard to this day.

Escape in Arizona

Of all the German naval officers of World War II, few were as clever and daring as Capt. Jürgen Wattenberg. He had once been the navigation officer of the battleship *Graf Spee*. After that vessel was sunk, Wattenberg was imprisoned by the British in Argentina, but he soon escaped and made his way back to Germany.

Greeted as a hero, Wattenberg was given command of a submarine. Late in 1942, Wattenberg's sub, while operating in the Caribbean, was sent to the bottom by British destroyers.

Wattenberg and most of his officers and crew members ended up as prisoners of the British on the Caribbean island of Trinidad. Later, the British handed them over to the Americans, who put them in prisoner-of-war camps in the United States.

That was not unusual. During World War II, Germans and Italians captured in combat were often sent to the United States for imprisonment. In fact, from 1942 through 1945, nearly half a million enemy soldiers and sailors were held prisoner in some five hundred camps in forty-five states.

A prisoner-of-war camp was usually part of a military base. Prisoners were kept in the base stockade, which was divided into smaller fenced-in areas called compounds.

Prisoners who could be trusted were put to work. They picked fruits and vegetables and cut wood. They worked in base mess halls and laundries. Prisoners who performed such chores were paid eighty cents a day.

After his arrival in the United States, Jürgen Wattenberg was moved from one prisoner-of-war camp to another. He proved a troublemaker at each. His appearance never failed to lead to rioting and bloodshed. Americans called Wattenberg a "Super Nazi."

When accused of causing unrest, Wattenberg always claimed to be innocent. Prison officials were never able to prove him guilty of any misdeeds.

Early in 1944, Wattenberg was transferred to Papago Park, a prisoner-of-war camp located amidst the scrub cactus and barren hills of south-central Arizona. Papago Park housed nearly 3,500 German naval officers and seamen.

Just to the north of the camp was Camelback Mountain, a well-known landmark. The skyline of the city of Phoenix could be seen in the distance.

At Papago Park, Wattenberg had one goal: cause the Americans as much trouble as possible. He refused to use English when speaking with any of the Americans. He would not attend any of the camp movies, take educational courses, or accept any of the other privileges that were offered.

Wattenberg branded as a traitor any German prisoner who worked for the Americans. He never stopped complaining about the treatment he was receiving.

Camp officials thought it would be a good idea to separate Wattenberg and thirty or so of the other troublemakers from the rest of the men. Compound 1-A was established for them.

Almost as soon as Wattenberg and the others arrived at Compound 1-A, they began making plans for a mass escape. Their idea was to break out through a long tunnel they would dig. Once they were free, they would make their way to Mexico, a hundred or so miles to the south.

Digging the tunnel became a great challenge for the prisoners in Compound 1-A. Said one later: "It was a kind of sport. We lived, ate, slept, talked, whispered, and dreamed 'tunnel,' and thought of little else for weeks on end."

Choosing where the tunnel should end was a simple matter. Beyond the second of two fences that surrounded the camp stood an electric-light pole in a clump of bushes. The tunnel should end near the pole, the men decided. They determined the pole to be 178 feet from the tunnel entrance.

Just behind the camp bathhouse was where the prisoners decided to locate the tunnel entrance. The bathhouse was where the prisoners took their showers and washed their clothes.

About ten feet from the bathhouse was a big coal box, about five feet high. Along with the bathhouse itself, the coal box would help to hide the tunnel entrance from the guards. As an added safeguard, the prisoners strung a rope from the coal box to the bathhouse, then used it to hang clothing out to dry.

In the coal box were small, short-handled shovels. They were intended for filling pails with coal, to be carried to the small stoves in the barracks where the prisoners lived.

Using the shovels, the prisoners first dug a hole six feet deep. This was the tunnel's entrance shaft. Besides the shovels, the prisoners had also gotten their hands on a small, short-handled pick.

Once the entrance shaft was completed, they began digging the horizontal tunnel through which the escape would be made. the tunnel was 2½ feet in diameter, or just big enough for a man to crawl through.

The diggers worked in groups of three. One man worked at the head of the tunnel with the shovel and pick. The second man was behind him. His job was to fill a pail with the excavated soil (the same pail that prison authorities had provided for hauling coal). The second man passed the pail to the third man, who was stationed at the tunnel entrance. He emptied the pail and gave it back to the second man. He also served as a lookout.

Diggers worked only at night and for only ninety minutes at a time. The first group of three men worked from eight o'clock to nine-thirty; a second group from nine-thirty to eleven, and a third, from eleven to twelve-thirty. At twelve-thirty, digging ended for the night.

The soil, called caliche, although hard-packed, usually crumbled fairly easily when hacked at with the shovel or pick. Some nights the tunnel advanced by as much as two or three feet. But other times the tunnelers came upon rocky sections. Then it was possible to excavate only a few buckets of soil for that night.

As the tunnel got longer, the prisoners built a small four-wheeled cart to haul the dirt out. The man digging at the head of the tunnel would fill the cart. The second man, stationed at the other end, would pull the cart toward the entrance and empty it. The first man would then pull it back and load it up again.

The prisoners swiped electric wiring, sockets, and bulbs to light the tunnel. For electric power, they simply plugged the tunnel wire into a bathhouse socket.

One problem the tunnelers faced was how to keep the tunnel straight and level. It was easy for the man doing the digging to veer to his right or left or up or down without even realizing it.

One of the prisoners provided a simple device that helped to keep the tunnel almost arrow-straight. Using melted wax, he anchored two candles of the same height a few inches apart on a large dinner plate. A third candle he mounted on a second plate.

By placing water in the first plate to be sure it was level, and sighting through the two flames toward the third candle burning in the distance, one could get an idea of how the digging was going. While the instrument helped to prevent the tunneler from straying from the course, the completed tunnel did have a few gentle turns and bends in it.

The biggest problem the tunnelers faced was what to do with the dirt. If they were to leave piles of dirt around, the guards were sure to get suspicious.

They tried many tricks. They scattered dirt in the prison flower beds. They flushed dirt down the toilets and wrapped it in bundles and stored the bundles in empty attics in buildings around the compound.

But as the nightly digging continued, more and more dirt began to accumulate. It was obvious that better methods were needed. Otherwise, the digging operation would have to be halted.

Two former submarine commanders, Fritz Guggenberger and Jürgen Quaet-Faslem, solved the problem. Both men were among the leaders in the escape attempt.

The idea came to them one hot Sunday afternoon. Most of the prisoners were in their barracks, resting, chatting, or playing cards — anything to escape the heat.

Guggenberger and Quaet-Faslem met in a shaded area out of the barracks to try to figure out what to do with all the dirt. Quaet-Faslem looked out over the criss-crossing rows of wire fences that divided the camp into its various enclosures. "Fritz," he asked, "shouldn't we have a sports area in this compound?"

Guggenberger looked at his friend quizzically.

"I'm serious," Quaet-Faslem said. "We should have a level spot in Compound 5. We could use it to play faustball occasionally. The guards call the game volleyball, I believe.

"Here we have nothing. The ground is too rough. It needs to be leveled out over there by Compound 5."

"Needs to be leveled out," Guggenberger said. "That's it, Jürgen! If we go to work creating a sports area, dirt gets moved about, then tunnel dirt can be brought there. Wonderful!"

Later that afternoon, Guggenberger and Quaet-Faslem met with the other two leaders, Hans Kraus and August Maus. They explained their plan. Maus applauded the idea but Kraus was skeptical. "It's too obvious," he said. "The Americans are sure to get suspicious when they see all that loose dirt lying around."

But Kraus agreed to meet with Lt. William S. Watson the next morning. Watson was in charge of Compound 5.

Watson thought that building a faustball field was an excellent idea, provided Col. William A. Holden, the camp commander, agreed. Watson even promised to provide the prisoners with two shovels and two rakes. Of course, he explained, the tools would have to be turned over to the guards at the end of the day. And the camp engineer, Lt. Thomas V. Jackson, agreed to truck several loads of dirt to the site to speed up the work.

Colonel Holden was just as pleased as Lieutenant Watson when the idea was presented to him. He gave his approval immediately because it sounded like a good way to keep the prisoners occupied.

Not long after, some thirty prisoners gathered at Compound 5 for a special ceremony marking the start of operations. The men cheered and applauded as Jürgen Wattenberg, using one of the new shovels, lifted the first shovelful of soil. About half of the men knew the true purpose of the faustball field. They did all they could to conceal their glee.

The method of getting rid of the dirt from the tunnel soon fell into a routine.

The prisoners working on the field had quickly created a tall pile of dirt. Each night, shortly after dark, a silent crew of prisoners secretly spread the dirt from the pile around the faustball field.

Still later that night, the tunnel diggers hauled new dirt from the tunnel over to Compound 5 and formed another dirt pile of the same size and shape. The new pile was formed at exactly the same spot where the previous one had stood.

Work continued in that fashion night after night. American guards and officers got used to seeing a pile of dirt sitting on what was to become a volleyball court. But they never realized it was a fresh pile of dirt every day.

Meanwhile, there were other problems to be solved. What about food? Once the prisoners had made their escape, what would they have to eat?

The four leaders met to discuss the topic. They agreed that they could get chocolate and black bread from Red Cross packages and stuff their pockets with it. They also agreed they needed some additional food item, something that would last two or three weeks.

Kraus had a suggestion. "We could toast American bread," he said, "break it up into small pieces, and package it tightly, so it wouldn't spoil. For a meal, we could mix it with water or milk."

It didn't sound very appetizing but the others agreed it would be nourishing and easy to carry.

Guggenberger had an added suggestion. "You know those little breakfast-food boxes we get, the individual-size ones? We could save those boxes, fill them with crumbled-up bread, and reseal them."

Everyone thought that was a good idea. They would begin to save cereal boxes.

During the meeting, they decided that only those doing the digging and helping to distribute the dirt would be allowed to use the tunnel to escape. And, further, those escaping would be divided into pairs or groups of three. Each pair or three-man group would be responsible for its own food, clothing, and other items.

All groups would travel by night and rest during daylight hours. It was agreed they would move across open country, avoiding cities. It would be foolish for thirty or so men dressed in strange clothing and speaking with foreign accents to suddenly show up in Phoenix at one time.

A date was set for the escape, too. "It should be a weekend or a holiday," said

Guggenberger. "How about Christmas? This place will fall apart then."

The leaders agreed. The break would be made at Christmastime, when camp rules and regulations were sure to be relaxed. "Merry Christmas! Merry Christmas!" the four men said to one another, and they laughed heartily and clapped each other on the back.

The last weeks of tunneling were the most difficult. Although the diggers had grown in skill and tended to work harder as the end drew near, they had to allow for a drainage ditch that crossed above the tunnel.

To avoid the drainage ditch, the tunnel had to go several feet deeper. They knew that if they broke through into the ditch, the tunnel would quickly flood. Months of hard work would be wasted.

About a week before Christmas, Wattenberg and the other leaders had the tunnel measured. It was 178 feet long. They had gone far enough.

But they wondered if the tunnel end was at exactly the point they wanted it to be. Guggenberger and Quaet-Faslem decided to conduct a test to find out.

In the bathhouse was a poker, a long metal rod used for poking or stirring the coal fire. Quaet-Faslem took the poker, and Guggenberger took a long stick with a rag tied to one end, and they crawled the length of the tunnel.

When they reached the end, Quaet-Faslem took the poker and used it to drive a hole upward through the tunnel roof. Fresh air rushed in through the opening when he removed it. The two men filled their lungs.

Then Guggenberger inserted the flag into the hole and pushed the stick upward. When the stick was all the way in, the two men waited. Nothing happened. Then all of a sudden they heard cheers. Men who had been posted on the roof of one of the barracks had seen the flag. It had come up almost exactly where they had hoped it would.

Walter Kozur was assigned to camouflage the tunnel opening. He built two shallow boxes out of scrap lumber. Each was about a foot-and-a-half long and a foot wide. When propped up side by side from the inside of the tunnel, they fit perfectly over the point of exit.

Kozur filled the boxes with dirt. He planted tufts of grass in the dirt and watered them regularly. The grass grew nicely. Later he planned to add leaves and twigs to the boxes so his creation would blend in better with the surrounding ground cover.

Two other prisoners had been given the job of preparing identification papers for those who planned to escape. No one in the compound had a camera or any way to obtain film. And even if they did, there was no way to develop film. That didn't matter. The Americans were eager to have it known back in Germany how well the prisoners were being treated. So they frequently snapped photographs of the prisoners and gave them to the prisoners to send to relatives at home. But the photos were never mailed. They were pasted onto documents meant to look like passports.

Official-looking stamps were cut from leather and rubber scraps.

The prisoners scheduled their escape for Saturday, December 23, 1944. They waited quietly through the day until darkness fell.

Quaet-Faslem and Guggenberger were the first to go. Other groups followed every twenty minutes. In all, a total of twenty-five men made the break.

Quaet-Faslem and Guggenberger joked with the other prisoners as they climbed down the ladder at the tunnel entrance and disappeared beneath the surface. For the next half hour or so, they slithered along on their elbows, bellies, and knees, resting every few minutes. "Hurrah!" said Guggenberger when they reached the exit ladder at the end.

They climbed out, keeping hidden by the bushes near the tunnel exit. Then they headed out into the night.

Those who came after followed the same routine. While they all had the Mexican border as their chief goal, the immediate aim of most was to get as far away from Papago Park as possible and find a safe place where they would be able to rest the next day.

Papago Park authorities discovered the absence of the twenty-five prisoners the day after the escape. A huge army of searchers was organized to track them down. The search group was made up of security personnel from Papago Park, agents of the Federal Bureau of Investigation, officers of the Arizona Highway Patrol, and sheriff's deputies. Authorities also called upon the Papago Indians, who lived in the area, for assistance.

Arizona daily newspapers printed photos and descriptions of each of the men who had escaped. Thousands of people carried the photos in their pockets and were thus able to lend a helping hand to the search.

During the last days of December and into the early weeks of January, most of the escaped prisoners followed the strategy of hiding out by day and hiking south toward Mexico at night.

But a few of the escapees turned themselves in after only a brief period of freedom. Being cold and hungry in the Arizona desert was no fun. They preferred the comforts of Compound 1-A at Papago Park.

One of the security patrols came upon Quaet-Faslem and Guggenberger while they were sleeping. They turned the two men over to Papago Park guards. The pair had been free for two weeks and were only ten miles from Mexico when captured.

Wattenberg made his escape with two other men. Johann Kremer and Walter Kozur. The three did not go far. They holed up in a mountain cave, a site from which they could almost see Papago Park.

Wattenberg planned that the group would head south as soon as the excitement created by their escape had died down. But he kept postponing their departure.

Food was no problem for the trio. Before their escape, Kozur had made arrangement with prisoners on a work detail to leave food in an abandoned automobile near the camp.

Every few nights, either Kozur or Kremer would wind his way down the trail to the car, pick up the food that had been left there, and return. The plan went off without a hitch.

The three men made several trips to Phoenix, which was about a three-hour hike from their hideout. Kremer and Kozur even went to a Phoenix bowling alley one night. They were fascinated; they had never seen American-style bowling before.

A week passed, then another, then a third. Wattenberg and his two companions continued to live in the mountain cave.

In the meantime, the other prisoners were being rounded up. Six were captured almost immediately after the break. Others were seized singly or in groups during the early part of January.

By the end of the month, Wattenberg, Kozur, and Kremer were the only prisoners still on the loose. Then Kozur was stopped on McDowell Road, about two and one half miles from Papago Park. After being questioned, he was taken into custody.

Kremer was captured shortly after. He had left the shelter of the cave to seek food from the abandoned car. As he opened the car door, he heard a strange noise. Just as he turned, he was caught in the bright beam of a flashlight. He could barely make out the three American soldiers who were facing him. Two held rifles to his head.

That left Wattenberg as the only escaped prisoner still at large.

When Kremer and Kozur did not return to the cave, Wattenberg felt certain they had been captured. He realized he was now alone.

On January 27, he ate his last bit of food. He knew he could not risk going to the old car. Doing that had cost Kremer his freedom, he figured.

Late in the afternoon, Wattenberg headed into Phoenix. He had only seventy-five cents in American money. He went to a restaurant and ordered a bowl of oatmeal with raisins and a pot of tea.

Later he approached the foreman of a street-cleaning crew and asked directions to Van Buren Street, one of the main streets in Phoenix. The foreman was puzzled by the question. "This is Van Buren Street," he replied. "You're standing in it."

The incident aroused the foreman's suspicions. A policeman happened to be passing by, and the foreman told him about the conversation and pointed Wattenberg out to him.

The policeman caught up to Wattenberg.

"Excuse me, sir," the policeman said. "Where do you live?"

Although startled by the sudden appearance of the policeman and the question, Wattenberg had a ready answer. "I'm a rancher in town for the weekend."

"Yes, sir," said the officer. "Where do you live?"

"In Glendale."

"Is that Glendale, Arizona, or Glendale, California?"

"Why, Glendale, back east."

"Sir, could I please see your Selective Service registration card?"

Wattenberg had no such card. He was hooked, and he knew it. He sighed. "I might as well tell you," he said, "I'm the man all you fellows have been looking for. I am Captain Jürgen Wattenberg, the escaped prisoner of war from Papago Park."

So ended what the Phoenix *Gazette* called "the greatest manhunt in the state's history." Today, where Papago Park was once located, there are bicycle paths, two golf courses, a picnic area, housing developments, and the Phoenix Zoo. The biggest, most sensational prisoner-of-war escape ever to take place on American soil is only a dim memory.

Nothing to Lose

It was just after daybreak on a gloomy, fog-filled April morning in 1944 at the Auschwitz concentration camp in southern Poland, time for morning roll call. The men in their striped uniforms spilled out of their barracks into the prison yard. The guards shouted loudly, ordering the prisoners to stand in straight lines.

When they had lined up, the guards counted them. One prisoner was missing. They counted again. Still missing.

Within seconds, alarm sirens began to scream. Guards shouted. Barking guard dogs were brought to the scene. In the prison commander's office, the telephones rang and rang.

A prisoner had escaped and the manhunt had begun.

No one knows for certain how many prisoners sought to escape from the horrors of Auschwitz. Many hundreds, probably.

The numbers who were successful can be counted on the fingers of one hand. This is the story of one of them — Siegfried Lederer.

The Holocaust, the mass murder of six million European Jews by the Nazis during World War II, began as the German army moved east into the Soviet Union in the summer of 1941.

The Nazis also killed many members of other ethnic groups, chiefly Gypsies and Poles. But only the Jews were marked for total destruction.

As the German armies advanced, Jews were driven into special areas called ghettos. They were kept there until they were crowded into cattle cars and transported to concentration camps. At the camps, most were treated as slave labor until they died of exhaustion or were murdered.

Auschwitz (now Oswiecim) was one of the most dreaded of the concentration camps. About thirty miles from Poland's border with Czechoslovakia, Auschwitz was opened in June 1940. The following year, the first huge gas chambers were installed. The camp soon became the Nazis' chief killing center.

After the war, a director of the camp testified that more than 2½ million men, women, and children were gassed to death at Auschwitz. Another half million died of starvation and disease.

Siegfried Lederer arrived at Auschwitz late in 1943. Lederer had belonged to a Czech resistance group that sabotaged key industrial plants aiding the Nazi war effort. After his role in these acts of destruction was discovered, Lederer was seized and imprisoned at Theresienstadt, a Jewish ghetto in Czechoslovakia.

One day, some two thousand men, women, and children were taken at gunpoint from Theresienstadt and herded into railroad boxcars for the journey to Auschwitz. Lederer was one of those seized.

Before the train left, Lederer's identification papers were stamped with the initials RU, for *Rueckker Unerwuenscht*, the German words for "Return Unwanted." Lederer's fate was sealed. RU meant he would never leave Auschwitz alive.

The train carrying Lederer and the other prisoners arrived at Auschwitz on a cold December morning in 1943. When the car doors were flung open, Lederer caught a glimpse of tall barbed wire fencing stretching in every direction. Prison guards waited as the prisoners were ordered from the cars. Each guard had a fierce-looking dog on a leash.

SS officers, members of the special police force of the Nazi Party, stood to one side. They held heavy clubs and were armed with pistols.

The prisoners were ordered to line up in columns of five. Then they were marched into the camp.

Lederer walked with his friend Miroslav Zeimer. Beyond the barbed wire fences, they saw prisoners dressed in tatters. Some wore paper bags, which had once held cement, as coats. Others had their feet wrapped in rags.

They passed a women's camp. There they saw creatures with shaved heads. They did not look like women.

Inside the camp, Lederer saw a wooden cart loaded with heavy stones that was being pulled by a dozen half-starved men hitched to the cart like horses. A guard with a whip sat on top of the stones.

The prisoners from Theresienstadt passed through the gates of the camp where they were to live. A dirt road divided the camp in two. On each side of the road were several barracks, long huts with tarpaper roofs. They had no windows, only small square openings with overlapping slats. In the middle of the camp stood a tall watchtower manned by a guard behind a machine gun.

The procession halted. An SS officer addressed the prisoners. "All those who arrived today will occupy these barracks," he said. "Men will live on the left side, women on the right. The children will have a block of their own."

Some people complained, but no one asked for special treatment.

Then came an order: "Line up. Food is ready."

Every prisoner got a bowl of turnip soup and two pieces of bread.

Next, the prisoners were ordered to line up for registration. When it became Lederer's turn to register, the clerk looked at his card, turned to a supervisor, and said, "A special case."

The supervisor examined the card. He noted the many times that Lederer had been found guilty of anti-Nazi activities and the names of the prisons in which he had been held. On Lederer's card he wrote the words, "Dangerous: political."

"You have been lucky," the supervisor said to Lederer. "But wait, we'll show you."

The prisoners were ordered to take off their clothes, except for their underwear. They were given striped uniforms in exchange.

Then they were forced to hand over their watches, rings, and any other valuables they carried. Lederer and Zeimer managed to keep their watches and pocketknives by hiding them in their shoes.

A number was tattooed on the left forearm of each prisoner. Lederer was given the number 170521.

The section of Auschwitz where the prisoners from Theresienstadt lived was known officially as B-II-b. But it was unofficially called the Czech family camp.

The Czech family camp was partly self-governed. While the most important posts were filled by Nazis, the prisoners were allowed to appoint their own people for certain duties.

Because Lederer spoke German, he was named a block man, that is, he was put in charge of the block — or barracks — in which he lived.

As a block man, Lederer had use of the block-man's hut, a small, crudely built shelter, which was meant to serve as an office. He used the hut to meet with his friends.

One day a column of trucks lumbered

into the Czech family camp. SS officers with machine guns guarded the trucks. Forty prisoners were loaded into each truck.

The prisoners in the trucks did not know where they were being taken. They did not know that the Nazis had chosen them for "special treatment." Special treatment was the term the Nazis used for killing Jews in gas chambers. The prisoners in the trucks were never seen again.

One day Lederer and Zeimer were chatting in the block-man's hut. As usual, the talk was of escape.

"We *must* escape," said Zeimer. "There is no risk in it. We are just living corpses anyway."

A knock came at the door. A prisoner entered and said that Lederer was to report to the guardhouse immediately.

Lederer grew pale. What did the SS guards want him for? He began emptying his pockets of all forbidden articles — his wristwatch and pocketknife, cigarettes, and a lighter. He put on his blue block-man's hat and left without saying a word.

Lederer ran all the way to the guardhouse. When he knocked at the door, he was greeted with silence. Slowly he pushed the door open. He sighed with relief to see

Viktor Pestek seated at a table in the center of the room. Although an SS officer, Pestek was known to be warm and friendly, rare qualities among the Nazis at Auschwitz.

Lederer removed his cap and stood stiffly as he reported his name and serial number.

Pestek looked sternly at Lederer, then picked up a file card from the table and began reading from it. "Siegfried Lederer. Treacherous behavior. Group sabotage in Plzen. An attempt to escape. RU — Return Unwanted."

Pestek handed the card to Lederer and pointed to the letters in a red circle. "Anyone who is RU is more or less dead," he said.

Lederer said nothing.

"Let me ask you something," Pestek said. "But you mustn't open your mouth about it." He glanced at a pistol resting before him on the table.

Lederer's heart pounded.

"If you could get across the border into Czechoslovakia, would there be anybody there to help you?" Pestek asked. "Would members of the underground hide you?"

Lederer's mind was racing. Was Pestek suggesting escape? Or was this a trap, a way to get him to reveal the names of members of the Czech underground? Lederer didn't know what to say. He kept silent.

Pestek pointed to the letters on the card again. "You have nothing to lose," he said.

Lederer thought hard. Prisoners often spoke well of Pestek. He was different from the other SS guards. And he was right when he said there was nothing to be lost in answering. He remembered what Zeimer had said, " 'We are just living corpses anyway.' " He decided to take the risk.

"I have good and reliable friends in Czechoslovakia," Lederer said. "They would help me."

"All right," said Pestek. "we will talk again."

Before Lederer left, Pestek warned him that he was soon to be summoned by the Gestapo, the German secret police. Gestapo officials wanted to know more about the resistance group to which Lederer had belonged. "They will try anything to get information out of you," Pestek said.

Pestek's warning proved to be true. After morning roll call a few days later, Lederer was taken from the family camp by an armed guard and brought to the main camp at Auschwitz, and to a one-story red-brick building there that served as Gestapo headquarters.

Inside, Lederer's tattooed number was

checked and compared to the papers in his file. Then he was made to stand near a door with his face turned toward the wall. He could hear shrieking and sobbing inside the room. The door opened, and a beaten prisoner, blood streaming from his head, was led out.

Lederer was brought into the room and seated across a big table from an SS officer. A pistol and a whip lay on the table. The SS officer asked about the resistance group in Plzen. In particular, he wanted to know about a woman named Gitta Steiner, a key figure in the resistance movement. Lederer knew that Steiner was in hiding, but he made up his mind he was not going to reveal what he knew.

"Do you know Gitta Steiner?" Lederer was asked.

Lederer admitted that he did.

"Where does she live?"

"In Theresienstadt," said Lederer, seeking to mislead the officer.

"How do you know that?"

"I saw her there."

"You lie!" the officer roared, and he struck Lederer across the side of the head with the whip.

"Where is she hiding?" the officer asked again. "Speak!"

"I saw her in Theresienstadt," repeated Lederer, who was bleeding now.

The questioning continued. But Lederer would reveal nothing.

When the officer realized that he was not going to get any information out of Lederer, he said to him, "I want to show you something." He took Lederer to a small room. There, an unconscious prisoner hung from the ceiling by a chain lashed about his wrists. Lederer closed his eyes in horror.

"I have no more time for you today," the officer said to Lederer. "But the next time we meet, I think your memory will improve."

A few days after, Pestek went to Lederer's block-man's hut to meet with him. "They are going to call me again," Lederer said, referring to the Gestapo.

"It will be worse next time," said Pestek. "You should think of a way to disappear."

Lederer didn't know what to say. Germans who wore the skull-and-crossbones of the SS filled him with horror. Why should he trust Pestek? It could be a trap.

Pestek seemed to be aware of what he was thinking. "Maybe you don't believe me because of the uniform," he said. "But there is no need for you to be afraid. I am not a Nazi. I am not one of them."

Then Pestek told Lederer about his boyhood in Rumania, how he had been recruited by the SS troops, how he had been sent to the Russian front and wounded near Stalingrad, and then, after he had recovered, how he was ordered to Auschwitz to serve as a concentration camp guard.

"I do not want gold or money," Pestek told Lederer. "What I do want is your promise that you will help to hide me and another person whom I want to help."

"Who is that?" Lederer wanted to know.

"You will learn that when the time comes. I will come to see you in three days and we will talk again."

Pestek held out his hand and Lederer grasped it. "Let's be friends," said Pestek. "Let Viktor and Siegfried make an agreement — for life and death."

The next time they met, Pestek explained his plan. "You will escape in an SS officer's uniform," he said. Pestek explained that he could not steal a uniform but that he would get uniform cloth and the needed decorations. Pestek said he would also get Lederer a pistol.

In the weeks that followed, Lederer began trusting Pestek more and more. Often the two men talked like old friends.

Pestek revealed the reason for his escape plan. Pestek had fallen in love with Rene Karen, a young Jewish prisoner who was scheduled for "special treatment" by the Nazis. When he and Lederer were free, Pestek planned to come back to Auschwitz and liberate Rene and her mother, who was also a prisoner.

Once Lederer agreed to cooperate, plans moved ahead quickly. Pestek had a prisoner who was once a tailor sew an SS jacket and trousers for Lederer. A former shoe-maker made him shoes, a belt, and a leather holster for the pistol.

As each article was finished, Lederer hid it behind the wall in an empty washroom. He covered each one with the wood chips prisoners used when sweeping concrete floors.

One day Pestek rode into camp on a bicycle. He propped the bike up against the wall of Lederer's block-man's hut, took a briefcase from the handlebars, and went inside.

Lederer was waiting for him. Without saying a word, Pestek placed the briefcase on the table and opened the lid. A pistol and an officer's cap with the SS skull-and-crossbones emblem were inside. Lederer winced at the sight of the cap.

"You've got to get used to seeing that emblem," Pestek said. "It's the best disguise you can have."

Pestek picked up the pistol, emptied it of ammunition, and showed Lederer how to use it.

Late one afternoon early in April, Lederer spotted Pestek's bicycle leaning outside the block-man's hut. That was the signal. He had two hours to get ready.

After he had changed into his SS officer's uniform, Lederer took the bicycle, hung the briefcase that Pestek had given him from the handlebars, and mounted the seat. The bike was too tall for him. He slid off the seat and had to remount. Finally he got the bicycle moving.

When he reached the first guard post, a voice called out to him. "Halt! Who goes there?" It was Pestek.

"SS officer," Lederer replied. Pestek came out of the door, nodded, and then went back inside and told the guard to open the gate.

Pestek, who had been given permission to visit his sick parents in Rumania, said to the guard, "I'm going, too. My train leaves in half an hour."

The guard hurried down the steps to the

gate. When he saw Lederer, he saluted, unlatched the gate, and opened it. As they passed through, the guard said good-bye to Pestek and told him to enjoy his time off.

Lederer walked the bicycle as the two men made their way along the busy road leading to the camp's main gate. The lights of cars and other vehicles blinded them. Once they had to jump into a ditch to avoid being hit by a passing truck.

As they reached the end of the camp, they were suddenly caught in the beam of a watchtower spotlight. "Halt! Who goes there?" a guard's voice called out.

They stopped. Luckily, the guard recognized Pestek.

"Okay, Viktor, it's you," the guard said. "And who is that with you?"

"SS," said Pestek. "He's coming from our camp."

The guard gave a friendly wave and switched off the light. Lederer sighed in relief as the darkness closed about him again. "Pass," the guard said.

They went past an SS barracks and a hospital. Lederer put the bicycle in a stand in front of a small building that served as an SS canteen. Just ahead was the main gate and another guard tower.

"Halt! Who goes there?" a guard cried. He climbed down a ladder from the tower and came over and shined a flashlight in the faces of the two men.

"The password!" the guard demanded.

"*Tintenfass* [the inkpot]," they answered in the same breath.

"Pass!" said the guard, and he lifted the gate.

In the distance, Lederer could see an iron bridge leading to the railway station. The station meant freedom, he thought. He had to fight an impulse to run for it as fast as his legs could carry him. As they neared the bridge, they could see and hear a train coming into the station.

"That's our train!" said Pestek. "Let's go!" They raced across the bridge, arriving at the station as the train was preparing to depart.

Lederer couldn't believe what was happening. Civilians on the platform were freely getting on the train almost in the shadow of the barbed wire fences that enclosed the hell of Auschwitz.

Lederer and Pestek jumped onto the last car of the train and squeezed themselves in. The train started moving.

The car was jammed with civilians carrying bundles, boxes, and old suitcases. It was stuffy and smelly. As the two men made their way through the car, they could see the faces of peasant women in scarves and men in old caps. Some passengers lay in the aisle on their baggage. Others stood and talked in soft voices.

They moved into the next car. It also was packed.

Lederer noticed that people stopped talking whenever he and Pestek approached. It was the SS uniform. Lederer could feel the tension mount and see the hatred in the eyes that stared at them.

In a third car, the two men found a place to sit. Pestek explained that when the train stopped at the town of Cidice, they would change to an express train. The express would take them across the border at Bohumin.

"How will I cross the frontier?" Lederer asked. "I have no identification, no documents."

Pestek frowned. "We'll see what happens," he said.

When the train pulled into Cidice, Lederer's fears proved correct. Out of the window, they could see military police in their green uniforms, who were stopping everyone — enlisted men, officers, and civilians — to examine their identification papers. Pestek was grim-faced. His plans had not included how to cope with the military police.

The car emptied quickly. Pestek watched

out the window and wondered what to do.

Just then an express train came rolling along into the station and ground to a stop. As the passengers began getting off, they were halted by the military police and asked to produce their identification papers.

The next to last car of the express train was a mail car. Suddenly Pestek had an idea. "Come on!" he called to a worried Lederer. "Let's go!"

The two men dashed across the platform and boarded the express train. The military police on the platform were too busy with the passengers who had just arrived to bother with the two SS officers in black boots and carrying briefcases.

Pestek and Lederer hurried through the train to the mail car, which was manned by two clerks in blue uniforms. *"Heil Hitler!"* Pestek called out, raising his right hand. the two clerks snapped to attention.

Pestek explained that they were there to inspect the parcels and suitcases. The clerks stepped back meekly.

Pestek and Lederer began sorting through the boxes. Some they called "suspicious" and opened them. When they found nothing of importance, they ordered one of the clerks to "Wrap it up again."

The clerks were puzzled by the SS men. No inspection had ever taken place before. But the clerks didn't think it would be wise to interfere.

After writing down the names and addresses of a few parcels, and setting them to one side, Pestek announced that they were finished. The two men left the mail car and found a seat in another car, where they were able to sleep until daybreak. When the train reached Olomouc, they moved into the dining car and had breakfast.

The two men remained aboard the train until it arrived at Prague, Czechoslovakia's capital and largest city. They scanned the platform before leaving the train. There were no military police checking papers.

At a second-hand shop in Prague, Lederer sold a gold bracelet he had brought with him. Then he bought a second-hand suit, shirt, tie, shoes, cap, and underwear. At a public bath, Lederer changed into the civilian clothes.

Pestek remained in uniform. He was, after all, officially on leave. His name was not yet connected with Lederer's.

Later in the day, the two men went back to the railroad station and boarded a train to Plzen, a large Czech city about fifty miles to the west. Lederer believed he would find friends to help them there.

In the meantime, back at Auschwitz, Lederer's absence had been discovered at morning roll call. At just about the same time that the train carrying Lederer and Pestek was drawing into the station at Prague, Gestapo headquarters in Auschwitz was sending a printed message to all Gestapo offices in Germany and Czechoslovakia. The message read:

SIEGFRIED LEDERER, JEWISH PRISONER IN PROTECTIVE CUSTODY, ESCAPED AT NIGHT, APRIL 5, 1944, FROM CONCENTRATION CAMP AT AUSCHWITZ. ALL INVESTIGATIONS SO FAR UNSUCCESSFUL. START SEARCH IMMEDIATELY.

Lederer's photograph was taken from the files, copied, and sent to Gestapo offices throughout Germany and Czechoslovakia, to German and Czech police stations, and to all frontier command posts.

Lederer knew the tactics that the Gestapo would use in attempting to track him down. He realized that the Gestapo would be watching all of his friends and relatives, and he would have to avoid contact with them. But there was one woman he was relying on for help. Her name was Gitta Skala. She was a member of the Czech underground. The Gestapo knew nothing about her.

Not long after the two men arrived in Plzen, Lederer went to a pay telephone and called Skala. The two agreed to meet at Skala's apartment.

"What do you need most?" Skala asked Lederer and Pestek.

"We need a lot," Lederer said. "Identity cards and papers, money and shelter."

Skala explained that she was in contact with an engineer in Prague who could provide them with false papers. His work was so skillful that it fooled even experienced SS officials. Skala said she would go to Prague with Lederer and Pestek and introduce them to the man.

Once they had been provided with proper identification papers, Pestek began pressing Lederer to go back to Auschwitz to rescue Rene. Lederer agreed to do so.

Again they disguised themselves as two SS officers. In Prague, they boarded the international express for the return trip. Pestek carried with him a letter in the name of a Gestapo official ordering him to take two women prisoners out of Auschwitz for questioning.

They traveled without any problems. In

Cidice, they changed from the express to a local train to Auschwitz.

Once aboard the train, they agreed to part briefly upon reaching Auschwitz so that Pestek could visit a friend in the nearby town of Myslowice. Lederer warned Pestek that it was not a good idea, but he insisted.

"I'll be back from Myslowice tomorrow," Pestek said. "Meet me at the night train."

Lederer stayed overnight in a hotel in the town of Auschwitz. In the evening, he went to the station to meet the train from Myslowice.

Not long before the train arrived, Lederer heard the roar of motorcycles. They stopped in front of the station. They were driven by SS soldiers.

The squad of SS men forced those waiting for the train to go inside the station. Then they sealed the station doors. Lederer's heart was racing. The SS troops took positions on the platform.

The train from Myslowice was approaching in the distance. As it rattled into the station, Lederer could see Pestek at a window. Pestek seemed to be looking for him.

The commander of the SS squad jumped onto the step of Pestek's car. Then Lederer heard a shot. People screamed.

Lederer took advantage of the confusion to flee. He made his way to Bohumin, where he took a train back to Prague.

Lederer had no way of finding out what happened to Pestek. However, he felt certain that Pestek had been betrayed by the friend that he had gone to see in Myslowice.

Lederer heard rumors that Pestek had been tortured and killed by the SS. An Auschwitz survivor confirmed the rumors after the war.

Lederer, after a brief stay in Prague, returned to Theresienstadt. He later became a member of a resistance group that fought the Nazis.

After the war, Lederer was decorated for his deeds. He married and led a quiet life with his wife and son in a suburb of Prague.

Lederer's story was told in rich detail in the book *Escape from Auschwitz* by Erich Kulka. The book was first published in Czechoslovakia in 1966 and later in the United States.

Lederer died at the age of sixty-eight on April 5, 1972. The date was exactly twenty-eight years after his extraordinary escape from Auschwitz.

One Time, Two Times

At a point about twenty miles south of
Rome where two dusty roads met, Lt.
Walter Granecki sat on a big rock behind
thick shrubs and started making notes on
a map. Granecki and Lt. Carl Pennington
had just finished a road search for mines
and enemy soldiers.

They found neither. Now they planned
to tell headquarters it was safe for American tanks and heavy vehicles to move into
the area.

It was May 26, 1944, almost a year before the German armies occupying Italy
were to surrender to the Americans. The
day was sunny and warm. The clean air
smelled good.

Suddenly Granecki heard a snakelike
hiss and swung around. Pennington was
crawling toward him.

"Pssst!" Pennington said again, and jerked a thumb over his shoulder.

About twenty-five yards up a narrow path was a German soldier. He was wearing camouflaged battle dress. In his hands he held a burp gun, a type of submachine gun. He started walking down the path toward Granecki and Pennington.

"Let's grab him!" Granecki whispered. Pennington nodded, then poked the barrel of his submachione gun through a bush. Granecki got down on his belly and started circling around to get in back of the German.

He had hardly gotten started when he glanced back and froze at what he saw. A second German soldier had appeared in back of Pennington. He, too, had a burp gun.

"Psst!" Granecki said to Pennington, and pointed. "I'll take care of the guy in back of us," he whispered. "You keep an eye on the other one." Pennington nodded.

Still lying flat, Granecki propped himself up on one elbow and took careful aim at the German soldier who was ambling down the path. When the soldier was about five yards from him, Granecki shouted, "*Achtung!*"

The stunned German soldier swung

around to face Granecki. But he didn't drop his gun.

Granecki counted to three and was about to pull the trigger when he felt Pennington tug at his arm. "Look behind you," Pennington said.

Coming out of the field behind them were six or seven German soldiers, all with burp guns ready to fire. When one of the Germans spotted Granecki, he shouted, *"Achtung!"* then added, "Hands up!" At the same time, all of the Germans, including the one Granecki had been covering, took aim at the Americans.

Granecki's heart sank. He knew immediately that he and Pennington were prisoners of war.

The Germans disarmed the two Americans, then searched them. They took Granecki's billfold, which contained snapshots of his wife, Juanita, and his baby, Ronald Lee. Granecki had never seen his son. He had been born while Granecki was overseas.

Motioning with their guns, the Germans marched the two Americans almost a quarter of a mile to a wine cellar. They went down a long, winding flight of stairs. At the bottom, seated on the floor amidst stacks of wooden wine barrels, were about a hundred German soldiers. At the sight of so many Germans, Granecki lost all hope of rescue or escape.

The Germans were nervous about what the Americans were planning, and they tried to get information from Granecki and Pennington. How many troops were in the area? What type of equipment did the Americans have? But Granecki and Pennington would give only that information they were required to give — name, rank, and serial number.

The Germans tried an assortment of tricks to get more information from the two. One questioner screamed at them. Another took a soft approach. "Look," he said, "life in a prisoner-of-war camp can be pretty tough. But we can make it a lot easier for you." Granecki and Pennington wouldn't even reply to the man.

In the days that followed, the Germans moved Granecki and Pennington from one prisoner-of-war camp to another. During one stretch, they slept five nights in five different camps.

They finally ended up at the Laterina camp, 125 miles north of Rome. It was one of the worst camps the two men had ever seen. Breakfast was a cup of tasteless coffee and nothing else. Lunch consisted of a cup of thin soup and bread. For the evening meal, the prisoners got thicker soup but no bread.

One morning just before dawn, Granecki, Pennington, and a number of other prisoners were rousted out of their beds and ordered into a truck. They spent thirty hours crammed together as the truck headed north.

The truck finally arrived at Mantova, an ancient city in northern Italy, about one hundred miles south of the Swiss border. There, a larger prisoner-of-war camp was located. No one had ever escaped from the Mantova camp.

Several days after arriving at Mantova, Granecki awoke in the middle of the night with a sharp pain in his right side. It was caused by a knife wound he had suffered many years before, and which had hospitalized him in the past. German doctors examined Granecki. They were suspicious he might be faking the pain, but when they realized he was serious, they ordered him to the prison hospital.

It was a lucky break for Granecki. A few days after he was hospitalized, Pennington and the other prisoners were shipped to Germany. In addition, Granecki was given better food in the hospital. He got milk for the first time in more than a year, and some fruit and cake.

As his pain began to respond to treatment, Granecki started to wander about the hospital corridors. A nurse questioned him. Granecki said he couldn't sleep at night, and that was why he was wandering about. The nurse gave him some sleeping pills. Granecki threw the pills away. He didn't care about sleeping. He wanted to learn all he could about the layout of the hospital. Escape was always on his mind.

An important railway terminal was located near the prison. Allied planes bombed it frequently. Whenever they did, the guards herded the prisoners into the hospital cellar. During one raid, Granecki discovered that one of the windows in the cellar had no bars. That could be a way out. Now Granecki began plotting more seriously.

There were some American and British soldiers in the prison who had escaped from other prisons and had been recaptured. But before their recapture, they had roamed the countryside. They explained that even though Italy and Germany were wartime partners, many Italian civilians supported the Allied cause. In fact, there were several bands of armed Italians in the area who were fighting the Nazis behind the German lines. They were called partisans. They welcomed escaped prisoners of war.

That was exciting news to Granecki. It boosted his confidence. Granecki began trading with other prisoners and some of the prison workers to obtain the clothing he would need once he got free.

An American lieutenant had given him a fountain pen. Granecki traded it for an extra pair of shoes. He also acquired a black shirt, a pair of gray civilian pants, and about thirty-five dollars in Italian money.

Then he got some workers in the prison hospital to give him lessons in Italian. In exchange, he started teaching them how to speak English.

On the night of August 14, Granecki decided to make the try. A little bit before midnight, he put on the shirt and trousers he had obtained. He put on his army uniform over them. Then he started for the unbarred window in the hospital cellar.

He tiptoed out of the ward when the nurse on duty was busy with another patient, then raced down a stairway leading to a main corridor. On his way, he spotted a Nazi guard lying on a wheeled stretcher. The guard was sleeping. By the time Granecki reached the cellar, he was soaked with sweat because of all the clothing he was wearing.

The cellar window was no problem. It was sealed with a wooden frame covered with burlap. Granecki lifted the frame out and set it down outside the window. He boosted himself up onto the window ledge and then crawled out on his belly.

There was no moon but the sky was filled with stars, which shed some light. Just ahead Granecki could see the seven-foot barbed wire fence that surrounded the hospital. Even though Granecki knew the area was not patrolled by guards, he crawled on his belly all the way to the fence.

When he reached it, he crawled along parallel to the fence until he came to a stone pillar, one of two that supported a heavy iron gate. Granecki climbed to the top of the pillar, then jumped down to the dirt road on the other side.

Thinking he was free, Granecki straightened up and started running. But he had gone only a short distance when he came upon a second fence. It was made of wire mesh and topped with barbed wire. At first he thought he was trapped. Then he thought he might be able to get over the fence's double iron gate.

He started climbing the gate, using the ornamental ironwork for footholds. He was only a few feet fom the ground when his foot banged against the gate and he felt something give. He looked down and saw that a small door set in the ironwork had swung open. Granecki dropped back down to the ground and walked through the doorway to freedom.

Granecki kept on the move all night long. He hurried through fields and vineyards, across highways and over railroad tracks. He wasn't quite sure in which direction he was headed, but he really didn't care. All he wanted to do was get as far away from the prison as possible.

When dawn came, Granecki lay down in a meadow. He saw a small village nearby. Between where he lay and the village was a big barn and a farmhouse. Granecki was very hungry, so he decided he would go up to the farmhouse and ask for something to eat. He knew he would be taking a chance, however. Although he remembered other prisoners had told him that most Italians would be friendly to any American, there were many who sided with the Germans and would look upon any American as an enemy.

As Granecki approached the house, an old man came out and began to yell at him.

Granecki couldn't understand what the man was saying. The man kept screaming at him. Maybe he thinks I'm a tramp, Granecki thought.

"American," Granecki said, pointing to himself.

The man stopped yelling, "Ah," he said. "Escaped?"

Granecki nodded.

The old man grinned and motioned for Granecki to wait. Then he went back into the farmhouse. Granecki thought the man was going to get him something to eat.

Suddenly an elderly woman came running out of the barn. She pointed excitedly in the direction the old man had taken. *"Tedeschi!"* she said. *"Tedeschi!"* Granecki knew the word meant "Germans." He realized that the old woman was telling him that the man was no friend, that he had gone to call the Germans.

"Go!" the woman cried. "Go!"

The woman didn't have to tell him a second time. Granecki dashed for some bushes nearby, peeling off his army uniform as he ran. He rolled it up and hid it under the bushes. Then he started up the road, half walking, half trotting. He hoped he no longer looked like an American prisoner of war.

Granecki kept walking all morning. He

wasn't concerned about which way he was heading because he wasn't yet sure how he going to complete his escape. He hoped to be able to go back through the Italian countryside to American lines. If that became impossible, he thought perhaps he might be able to make his way to Switzerland. Either way, he looked forward to finding bands of partisans who would help him.

Morning turned into afternoon. Granecki grew more tired and desperately hungry. But after his close call at the first farmhouse he had approached, he was afraid to ask for food or a place to rest.

Finally, he could stand it no longer and approached another farmhouse. He picked out the poorest one he could find because the Italian prisoners at Mantova had told him that the poorer the people, the more likely they were to be friendly to Americans.

A young woman with a small child was sitting outside the farmhouse. A second woman, much older than the first, was feeding chickens. There were no men in sight. Granecki approached the younger of the two women and said, "Eat."

The woman smiled, then let loose a torrent of words.

"No understand," said Granecki. "American."

The woman's mouth dropped open. "Ah, American," she said. Then, turning toward the older woman, she called out, "American! American!"

The older woman hobbled over and peered at Granecki.

"Parachutist?" she asked.

"No," said Granecki, "Prisoner. American." Then he pointed to his stomach and said, "Eat."

The two women motioned Granecki to go into the house and sit at the kitchen table. They brought him fresh figs, tomatoes, and bread. Between mouthfuls, Granecki kept saying, "Good" and "Thank you." When he left, they offered to give him money, although it was obvious that they were very poor.

The scene in the farmhouse was replayed over and over in every Italian home that Granecki approached during the next few days. One farmer, besides feeding him, provided him with a dark blue sports shirt. Granecki felt he was looking more and more like an Italian all the time.

At each friendly farmhouse, Granecki asked where the nearest band of partisans was located. No one seemed to have any information about them, or at least they would not reveal what they knew.

Finally, after more than a week of asking questions, Granecki met a farmer who said he would lead him to the local partisan group. For two days, Granecki followed the farmer through rugged mountain country. They finally came to the partisan hideout, a big barn overlooking a valley. Three machine guns were set up in the barn's hayloft. They covered a road leading past the barn.

The partisan band, twenty-one men, all heavily bearded, was led by a tall, thin man named Franco. He had served as a lieutenant in the Italian army. Franco promised Granecki plenty of action if he joined the partisan group. "Fine," Granecki said, "I'll stick around for a while."

Not long after, the group raided an electric power plant, chiefly to get arms and ammunition from the guards stationed there. The raid stirred up a hornet's nest. Franco was brought word that the Germans were sending two hundred troops into the area to hunt the partisans down. The Germans were armed with flamethrowers and short-barreled cannons called howitzers.

Franco knew his tiny band could be wiped out by the German troops. He ordered the group to disband. Each man would then try to make his own getaway.

Granecki decided to thread his way south. He slept in fields or haylofts. At least once a day, he'd take a chance and stop at a farmhouse and ask for food. Although the countryside was soon crawling with German soldiers, Granecki was able to give them the slip.

Granecki's one wish was to cross the battle zone and reach the American lines, then get word to his family that he was still alive. He wanted to hear American voices and eat American food. He began to hurry, traveling at all hours of the day and night, taking shortcuts through towns instead of circling around them.

Nobody looked at him suspiciously. Nobody asked him any questions. He began to believe that he would be able to walk all the way to the American lines, still some one hundred miles away, without being halted.

One day in the small town of Cremona, Granecki passed a command post that was manned by Italian soldiers. He paid no attention to them. He felt that he looked so much like an Italian workman that he didn't have to worry. He had passed dozens of Italian soldiers before without being bothered. He kept right on walking.

He had not gone far beyond the command post when he heard a soldier shout, "Civilian, halt!" When he turned around, Granecki gasped at the sight of several soldiers armed with rifles running toward him. His first thought was to run, but he knew if he did, he'd be shot.

"What is it?" he asked the soldiers. They didn't answer. Instead, they searched him. When they discovered that he had no identification papers and heard his foreign accent, they clapped handcuffs on him. Later Granecki learned that the Italians had been alerted to be on the lookout for soldiers who had deserted the German Army, and something about him had made the soldiers suspicious.

The Italian soldiers had no idea that Granecki was an escaped prisoner of war. They turned him over to the Germans, anyway.

Two German soldiers drove Granecki toward a prison camp. As the truck wound its way through the Italian countryside, the road began to look familiar to Granecki. Then his heart sank. It was the road to Mantova. He was going back to the very prison from which he had escaped two and a half months before. He'd never felt so gloomy in all his life.

The German sergeant in charge of receiving prisoners recognized Granecki. "Oh, you're back," he said. "Well, I hope you had a good time, because your good times are over."

Granecki's stay at Mantova was a short one. One morning, only a few days after he arrived, all the prisoners were awakened before dawn, lined up, and made to march to the railroad station.

There, a special train awaited them. The men were loaded into boxcars. The train then set off for a prisoner-of-war camp deep within Germany.

Granecki slumped against one wall of the crowded boxcar as the train sped north. His chin was on his chest. He had been free, he kept thinking, and then he had blundered. Now he was paying the penalty for being careless.

There were thirty-six prisoners in the boxcar. They were divided into two groups. Each group was sealed into an end of the boxcar by a barbed wire fence.

Behind the barbed wire were the boxcar doors, which were partially opened, and five German guards.

There were three small windows in each end of the car. The windows had a door that closed with a snap catch. Granecki opened one of the doors and found himself face to face with sturdy iron bars He

71

opened a second window. More bars. He didn't bother to open the third.

The train hurried toward Germany. The German guards chatted among themselves, paying no attention to the prisoners.

It grew dark. One of the guards lit an oil lantern and hung it from the ceiling of the car. The lantern cast eerie shadows as it swung to and fro.

It began to get chilly. A guard slammed shut the boxcar doors. One of the prisoners shut the two windows Granecki had opened.

Later the air got stuffy. "Open a window," one of the guards called out.

"Of course, my good man," said an English officer. He reached for the third window. A few seconds later, the same officer, with surprise in his voice, declared softly, "There are no bars on that window."

Granecki jumped to his feet. He watched to see whether the guards had understood what the officer had said. Apparently they had not.

Granecki walked over to the window and stuck his head out. The cold night air rushed at him.

On the outside of the boxcar, Granecki could see the steel railings and foot supports used by the trainmen for climbing the cars. There were no guards outside the train. The window was wide enough to enable him to slip through.

"This is it!" Granecki thought. He had escaped through an unbarred window once before. He would do it again.

Back in the car, Granecki told his fellow prisoners what he planned to do. Two English officers announced they wanted to go with him. One was named Trevor, the other Granecki called Shorty.

Granecki went first, backing out the window as other prisoners shielded him with blankets. It was a very tight fit. For a moment he didn't think he would be able to get his hips through. He had to take several pieces of bread out of his pockets in order to make it.

Once outside the car, Granecki moved from the footholds on the car in which he had been riding to those on the next car, to make room for the other two men. They all hung on desperately as the cold wind whipped at them. They could make out dark masses of mountains in the distance. There was a river on one side of the tracks and a highway on the other.

But they didn't know where they were. They might still be in Italy. Or they could have crossed the border into Austria. Or maybe they were beyond — in Germany. They had no idea.

Suddenly the train began to slow down. They thought that meant it was going to stop. They jumped.

Granecki tried to curl himself up in a ball and roll. He landed in a water-filled ditch. He kept perfectly still until the train was out of sight.

He found Trevor and Shorty nearby. Then the three of them set out on a dirt path leading away from the railroad track. The path led steadily upward into the mountains. It got cold. There were patches of snow. Then it began to rain, and the rain turned to sleet.

With dawn, they saw nothing but gray mountains strewn with rocks, shrubs, and a few stunted trees. They still didn't know where they were — in Italy, Austria, or Germany.

They walked all that day and the next night. They were freezing cold and starving.

On the morning of their second day of freedom, they came upon a small shack, "I wonder if it's safe," said Shorty.

"I don't care whether it is or not," Granecki said.

Trevor agreed. "You know," he said, "I believe I could put my arms around a German soldier and kiss him if he promised to give me food and shelter."

The three men were in luck. The shack was occupied by an old man and his wife. The man worked as a woodcutter. He told Granecki and his companions, to their great relief, that they were still in Italy.

The couple fed the three men. Afterward they collapsed on some straw and slept the entire day. At nightfall, they left. They walked all night. The next day, they found a group of houses with friendly Italians. They were fed and given warm clothing.

An English soldier was living with the families. He had escaped from a prison camp more than a year before and had been hiding out all that time. He told Granecki that he could get him a guide who would take him to the Swiss border. But Granecki didn't want to go to Switzerland. He wanted to get back to the American lines. It had now been six months since his first escape. He never stopped worrying about his wife, who had no idea whether he was dead or alive.

Granecki said good-bye to Trevor and Shorty and headed south again. The farmers in the area hated the Germans. Granecki had little trouble getting food and shelter. He traveled for two weeks without seeing a German soldier.

At one stop, a farmer gave him a letter for the leader of a band of partisans. The farmer said the partisans could help Granecki get through the battle zone to the American side.

When he got to the partisan stronghold, Granecki found forty men and eight women. Some of the men wore Italian uniforms, others had English uniforms. Still others wore German uniforms they had taken from soldiers whom they had killed or captured. It was a strange mixture.

The partisans controlled an area that was about ten miles square and located about twenty-five miles north of the battle zone. The Germans knew they were there but couldn't spare the troops it would take to storm the stronghold and capture it. The American forces were putting too much pressure on the Germans at the battlefront.

When Granecki presented his note to the leader of the partisans, he explained that he wanted to get through the battle zone to the American side. The partisan leader took Granecki's request in stride. "Okay," "we have a group starting tomorrow morning. You can go with it." Granecki could hardly believe his ears.

There were six in the group. The others were American airmen whose planes had been forced down in the mountains. They had parachuted to safety and been found by the partisans.

Just before they left, Granecki was told that they would be traveling through the mountains at night and it would be very cold. He was advised to wear a hat. When he wasn't able to find one, a partisan woman gave him a scarf, which he wrapped around his head.

As the group marched along, other groups joined them. When they had reached a point about fifteen miles north of the battle zone, they headed into the mountains. Sometimes the trail seemed to go straight up. There was snow and it was bitterly cold.

The battle zone was an area from three to five miles in width, with wide gaps between American and German positions. It was risky business to try to cross the battle zone without attracting fire from one side or the other.

Alongside a small bridge that spanned a mountain stream, Granecki spotted an American outpost. It consisted of a pair of machine guns that covered the road on which Granecki's group was traveling. "I'm an American," Granecki shouted in the direction of the machine guns. "I'm an American officer." The soldiers manning the guns kept them trained on Granecki and the others as they approached in case they were Germans trying to pull a trick.

One of the men took Granecki to his sergeant at a command post about fifty yards to the rear. The sergeant was feeding Granecki when the officer in charge of the unit, a lieutenant colonel, entered the room.

Granecki, out of habit, sprung to his feet and saluted. The colonel looked at Granecki and burst out laughing. He was wearing dirty, ragged civilian clothes, his shoes were in shreds, and about his head he wore the scarf the woman had given him. "What are you?" the colonel asked.

At that, Granecki started laughing, too. Then he explained who he was and how he happened to be there. When he had finished, the colonel picked up the telephone and called headquarters for food and medical supplies.

Suddenly Granecki realized that for the first time in six months he was back among Americans. He started to cry.

Not long after, Granecki was able to call his wife. When he told her who was calling, she didn't believe him. She thought someone was playing a cruel joke on her.

Granecki was finally able to convince her that it was no joke. He was alive, he was coming home, and soon — before Christmas. In that first telephone call, Granecki didn't bother to explain to her that he had been captured by the Germans, had managed to escape, had joined up with Italian partisans, and had made his way back to freedom. And that he had done it all twice.

Escape from the Japanese

When a man is forced to put down his arms and surrender, the war for him has reached an end. He becomes a prisoner of the enemy.

He realizes that he is not going to be living a life of comfort and ease. Yet he does expect decent treatment — food, clothing, shelter, and medical care. These basics are guaranteed by international agreements.

However, for the 65,000 men taken prisoner by the Japanese in the struggle to gain control of the Philippine Islands, the enemy provided a different set of rules. Humane treatment was the exception.

The Japanese spread the war to the Philippines within a few days after their attack on Pearl Harbor. It began when tens of thousands of Japanese troops invaded Luzon, the chief island of the Philippines.

As the invaders advanced, Gen. Douglas MacArthur, commander of the U.S. forces in the Far East, withdrew his troops to Bataan Peninsula in southwestern Luzon. MacArthur himself withdrew further — to Australia — vowing to return, but a shortage of food, ammunition, and medical supplies forced American and Filipino troops on Bataan to surrender early in 1942.

Corregidor, a rocky fortress in Manila Bay, held out for another month.

The prisoners the Japanese took at Bataan and Corregidor were forced to march seventy miles in the broiling heat to prison camps. This forced march became known as the Bataan Death March. About 10,000 Americans and Filipinos died from starvation or brutal treatment during the march.

This is the story of ten Americans who survived the Bataan Death March to become the first prisoners to escape from the Japanese in the Philippine Islands.

The ten men were lead by Comdr. Melvyn H. McCoy of the U.S. Navy. After their capture, McCoy and the others who were to become members of his group were marched to a prisoner-of-war camp at

Cabanatuan, about 75 miles north of Manila.

Cabanatuan was a place of torment. There was never enough food. Hundreds were beaten and tortured. Thousands died from sickness and disease. Death was the penalty for any attempt to escape.

In the fall of 1942, the Japanese decided to transfer about a thousand prisoners from Cabanatuan to another camp, this one near Davao City on Mindanao, the largest and southernmost of the Philippine Islands. The ship carrying the prisoners arrived at a Davao City pier on November 6, 1942. From the ship, the prisoners were marched seventeen miles to the Davao prison camp.

In the years before World War II, Davao prison had been operated by the Philippine Bureau of Prisons. About 2,000 convicts had been held there.

When the Japanese gained control of Mindanao, they transferred all but 150 of the convicts elsewhere to make room for the Americans. These 150 were kept at Davao prison to help run it. Though all of the prisoners were convicted killers, they were to prove kinder and more civilized than the Japanese.

At the Davao camp, the newly arrived

prisoners were lined up to be reviewed by the camp commanding officer. He was furious when he saw how many of them were seriously ill. He stormed about proclaiming he needed prisoners who were able to work hard, not a bunch of men so sick they could hardly stand.

"You have been used to a soft, easy life since your capture," the commanding officer told the prisoners. "All that will be different here. Now you will learn about hard labor. Every prisoner will be made to work until he is hospitalized."

The Davao camp was made up of dozens of barracks in which the prisoners lived. The barracks were ringed by barbed wire fencing. Outside the barbed wire were farms and plantations. Here, the men were put to work cultivating and harvesting rice, corn, and mung beans. Beyond the farms and plantations was the thick, steaming jungle.

For a time, the food at Davao was better than what the prisoners had been eating at Cabanatuan. While the basic food was still rice, the men were also served papayas, casavas, and bananas. And once each day, they were given a small portion of mung beans.

But in January, the Japanese suddenly

stopped giving prisoners fruits and vegetables. White rice — and only rice — was served at every meal.

The lack of good food caused many prisoners to fall sick. Some became ill with beriberi, a disease of the nervous system. Advanced cases of beriberi were sent to the hospital. These men sat all day rubbing their toes and fingers, which were wracked with pain. They could not sleep; they lost their appetites. They were pathetic to see. Other prisoners caught malaria. Yet there was no medicine available to treat them.

Early in January, Commander McCoy was put in charge of a thirty-man work force assigned to the prison's coffee plantation. Lt. Col. Steve Mellnik was named to assist him.

The men on the plantation worked six days a week, picking coffee and trimming the low-growing trees. If anyone in the camp happened to be caught stealing food, everyone had to work on Sunday, too.

One January afternoon, Commander McCoy returned to his barracks to be greeted by a sailor he had known before the fall of Corregidor. "It's Christmas, Commander!" the sailor shouted. "It's Christmas!"

McCoy's brow wrinkled. December 25th had passed several weeks before.

"It's Christmas!" the sailor said again. "Stuff from home. Boxes from the States. Red Cross boxes."

The news was true. Packages from the International Red Cross had arrived at the camp, two for each man.

The packages were filled with cheese, crackers, cookies, canned meat, cocoa, tea, and coffee. Best of all, they also contained medicines, including quinine, used in treating malaria.

Christmas had come late for the prisoners. But it was the most enjoyable Christmas any of them could remember.

The Red Cross food lasted about two months. Then the prisoners were put back on much the same rations as before — mostly meals of watery rice or soup.

Almost from the first day he had arrived at Davao, Commander McCoy began thinking about escaping. His plan was to slip away from the coffee plantation and plunge into the jungle, then make his way to the coast. There he would buy a boat or steal one and sail to Australia and freedom.

He knew his chances of success were not very good. But he also knew that if he remained in the hands of the Japanese for very long, he would die. Attempting escape was really the only choice.

McCoy had no intention of trying to escape alone. He knew he needed help. He began lining up others who wanted to go with him. He approached Lieutenant Colonel Mellnik, who was enthusiastic about the plan. Two sergeants — Paul Marshall and R. B. Spielman — also wanted to make the try.

"How far is Australia from here?" Marshall asked McCoy one day.

"It's more than a thousand miles to the nearest point," McCoy answered.

"And you mean, if we get through the jungle and get a boat, you can take us there?"

McCoy nodded. "Within ten or fifteen miles of any place on the map. Of course, we have to rig up some half-decent navigation equipment."

Lt. L. L. Boelens, another prisoner who joined the group, helped make a primitive sextant, a vital navigational device, from pieces of metal he found at the camp. The sextant is used in measuring the angular distance of the stars, sun, and moon. Boelens' sextant was hidden away until the day of the escape.

Beningno de la Cruz and Victorio Jumarung, two Filipino convicts, were added to the escape group. They offered to serve as guides, leading the Americans through the jungle to the coast.

Meanwhile, conditions in the camp kept getting worse. Many hundreds of prisoners, their bodies weakened by malaria, beriberi, and other diseases, were no longer able to work. They had to be removed to the prison hospital.

Beginning in the month of March, McCoy and other members of his group began sneaking packages of supplies and equipment out of the camp and hiding them at the edge of the jungle in the thick undergrowth.

Getting the bundles past the guards at the main gate was no problem once McCoy discovered that the guards could be bribed. When McCoy wanted to bring a package of supplies through the gate, he would place it in the bottom of a small cart, which was drawn by a water buffalo.

The package was hidden by covering it with firewood. On the back of the cart, McCoy hitched a bag of apples, which had been stolen from an orchard on one of the plantations. Only Japanese officers were allowed to eat apples, so the prisoners stole some to bribe the guards, who didn't ordinarily get that kind of food.

When the cart reached the sentry post,

McCoy handed the bag of apples to the guards. They waved the cart through the gate without bothering to inspect it.

McCoy and Mellnik set the last Sunday in March as the date for the escape. Sunday was the only day of the week that the prisoners were not forced to work.

The men planned to slip away right after morning roll call. Another head count was not scheduled until late afternoon. That meant the men would have several hours before their absence was discovered.

The week before the escape, the days dragged. Then the men got bad news. The Japanese had begun inspecting the canvas lunch bags carried by members of work parties leaving the prison. The guards were looking for forbidden food, such as fruit or vegetables.

On one such inspection, food had been discovered. The entire camp was to be punished by being made to work on Sunday, the same Sunday for which the escape was planned. McCoy had no choice but to postpone the attempt until the following Sunday and hope they would not be punished by an order to work again.

The day of the escape finally arrived. McCoy and the others awoke before dawn to make final preparations. McCoy first wrapped mosquito netting around his upper body. He knew it would be impossible to sleep in the jungle without protection from the netting.

He put on extra clothing under his regular clothing. He filled his pockets with food, precious medicine, and maps of the escape route, which he had drawn.

Getting through the main gate was the first problem the men had to solve. They had to be able to give the guard a good excuse in order to be permitted to leave the prison area on a Sunday to go out to the farms and plantations.

They decided it would be easier to divide themselves into two groups, five men to each. One of the groups would be headed by Marine Capt. R. C. Shofner, the other by McCoy.

During the work week, Captain Shofner supervised all the plowing done on the farms and plantations. This meant he was in charge of a herd of water buffalo, the animals used to pull the plows.

When Captain Shofner approached the sentry at the main gate, he explained that he and his men had to go to the farm to change the water buffalos' grazing area. The animals had eaten down the grass in the area where they were now grazing,

Shofner explained. It sounded believable. The guard signaled Shofner and his group to pass through.

Not long after, McCoy and his men approached the gate. The guard seemed puzzled. What did *this* group want?

McCoy's heart was pounding. He was worried about the extra clothing he was wearing and all the things he had hidden under his clothing. He was afraid his bulky appearance would make the guard suspicious.

"Where are you going?" the guard said sternly.

"I'm taking some of my men out to build a rain shelter on the plantations," McCoy answered. "With all the rain we've been having, we've been coming in soaked every night."

The guard looked at the group and the tools they were carrying. Without a word, he waved them through.

As soon as they reached the plantation, the men headed for the jungle to recover their equipmnet. But before they entered the jungle, they had to cross a prison road that was patrolled by a Japanese sentry. McCoy could see him approaching in the distance, his rifle slung over one shoulder.

McCoy formed his group into single file and marched them smartly along the road.

As they got close to the guard, McCoy ordered, "Eyes left!" Then he commanded, "Hand salute!"

The guard was impressed. Seldom did the Americans show the slightest respect for their Japanese captors. The guard grinned and returned the salute.

Shortly after, McCoy's group joined Shofner's. The men hurried into the jungle to recover the equipment and supplies they had hidden.

Jungle travel proved to be more difficult than anyone had expected. The mens' bodies were soon soaked from the terrible heat. Their ears were assaulted with the squawk of startled birds and the chatter of beady-eyed monkeys.

Soon they were in a swamp. They walked in water up to their knees. Sharp-edged coogan grass grew as high as their heads. They had to hack through it with big, heavy-bladed knives.

When darkness fell, the men were still in the swamp. The water was ankle deep.

To sleep that night, they made crude beds out of branches they had hacked from trees. They piled up the branches until each pile was above the water's surface. Then they and their blankets were able to stay dry as they slept.

But since they were at the point of exhaustion when they turned in for the night, each man fell into a deep sleep. No one awoke when the water rose during the night, and at dawn they were half floating.

Toward the end of the second day, the men heard the sound of rifle- and machine-gun fire in the distance. They knew immediately what that meant. The Japanese were on their trail. The gunfire was from a search party.

Two days later, they found evidence proving the Japanese were after them. They came upon a campsite and the remains of food that Japanese soldiers had eaten. They also found an empty ammunition clip for a .303 rifle.

After that, it was back into the swamps again. At one stage, the water was up to their armpits. They had to hold their bundles of food high above their heads as they sloughed through the water.

The deep water was not the worst of it. The water was infested with leeches, blood-sucking wormlike creatures that attached themselves to the men's flesh.

Sometimes there would be as many as a dozen leeches attached to one man's skin. Once a leech had fastened itself to the skin, it would suck blood, puffing itself like a tiny balloon. The only way to remove a leech was by prodding it with a lighted match or cigarette.

The men wore socks over their shoes and trouser cuffs in an effort to keep the leeches from getting to their skin. But some always got through.

The leech's bite is not harmful. But the puncture in the skin is an invitation to infection.

At the end of four days, the escape party had traveled only twelve miles, less than one third of the distance to the coast. But before the end of the first week, they had left the swampland and had begun traveling on open trails.

One day they spotted two armed Filipinos ahead on the trail. When the Filipinos realized that they had been sighted, they faded into the jungle.

Shortly after, the escape party came upon a small Filipino village in a jungle clearing. The men were warmly welcomed. Two of the natives said that they had been the ones they had seen in the jungle. They had fled, they said, because they thought the men were Japanese soldiers.

The worst part of the journey was over. No longer did the men have to endure a near-starvation diet. The Filipinos provided them with rice, eggs, cottage cheese, and coffee.

There was also carabao meat. The Filipinos would kill a carabao, or water buffalo, salt the meat heavily, cut it into strips, and hang the strips in the sun to dry. After twelve hours or so, the salted meat had dried. It could be kept almost indefinitely. Dried carabao meat became a staple of the men's diet for the rest of their journey.

The escape party now began traveling from one village to the next, with the Filipinos guiding the men through the thick jungle and rough terrain. They began making more rapid progress. Thanks to this fact, and their much-improved diet, the men's confidence soared.

When the men reached the coast, the Filipinos helped them obtain a small fishing boat. They loaded the boat with food, fuel, and supplies. Commander McCoy got out the sextant that had been stashed away many months before.

One steamy, moonless night, they left their dock and headed for the open sea and Australia.

When dawn broke, they gasped. Their small boat was chugging along just behind a pair of Japanese patrol vessels. Each was armed with a three-inch gun capable of blowing their tiny craft out of the water.

The men were afraid to turn back. Doing

so might arouse the suspicions of the Japanese. They simply continued to trail the two Japanese patrol vessels.

When the Japanese boats suddenly made an abrupt turn toward an inlet, the men did not follow. They continued on a course leading out of the harbor and toward freedom.

Their nightmare was over. The group finally reached Australia, and the Americans eventually returned to the United States. One man's journey to America was delayed, however. He fell in love with a Filipino woman and decided to remain in the Philippines until the war was over. The others, however, were reunited with friends and families.

In October 1944, troops under the command of General MacArthur returned to the Philippines and began clearing the island of Japanese forces. Within a few months, the Allies had regained control of the Philippines.

That was good news to McCoy and the other members of the escape group. They were also gladdened by V-J Day — August 15, 1945 — the day that Japan accepted Allied surrender terms, and all enemy resistance in the Philippines ended.

Incident at Cowra

In the summer of 1942, when Americans, Australians, and their allies went on the attack for the first time against the Japanese in the Pacific, they found themselves struggling against an enemy inspired by the ancient military code of Bushido. The Japanese fighting man was fanatical because of it.

Bushido stressed bravery and loyalty. Honor, in fact, was more important than life itself. The tradition of Bushido said that it was more honorable to die in battle than live as a captive and bear the shame of imprisonment. As a result, Japanese soldiers fought savagely, often resisting to the bitter end.

Being taken prisoner, on the other hand, caused the Japanese military man great shame. Prisoners felt they had dishonored their families.

The Japanese were shocked to learn that American prisoners actually asked to have their names sent home so that their families would know they were alive. Japanese prisoners tried to keep secret the fact that they had been captured. "We were dead men," a Japanese prisoner once said. "We had dishonored ourselves. Our lives were over."

The spirit of Bushido helped to trigger one of the biggest prison breaks of World War II. It was also one of the most tragic.

More than a thousand Japanese held prisoner in Australia rose up against their captors. It was a tragedy because 231 Japanese were killed in the uprising. Four Australian soldiers also died.

The Japanese, who occupied the island of New Guinea, hoped to use it as a jumping-off point for the invasion of Australia, which is just to the south. But late in 1942, Allied troops began to storm Japanese positions in New Guinea and Allied naval forces scored big victories in the waters south and east of the island. The tide of the war began to turn.

Japanese captured in the fighting for New Guinea were sent to a prison camp just outside the small town of Cowra, about 130 miles directly west of Sydney, Australia's largest city. The camp sat on a flat plain surrounded by low, tree-covered hills.

Almost circular in shape, the camp was divided by two wide roads that met at right angles at the very center. One of the roads had a heavy log gate at each end. Lights on tall poles kept the road very bright at night. The road was nicknamed Broadway.

The two intersecting roads divided the camp into four pie-shaped sections. Each was surrounded by two rows of barbed wire. In each section, there were twenty low, brown-painted barracks where the prisoners lived.

Italian prisoners who had been captured in North Africa occupied two of the camp's four sections. The fact that they were prisoners was not disagreeable to the Italians. They enjoyed their meals and comfortable living quarters. They were relieved that no one was shooting at them anymore.

The Italian prisoners often worked on farms near the camp, usually without being guarded. Some even lived with Australian farm families. Sometimes, when an Italian work party arrived back at camp late at night, they would find the big gate locked. The prisoners would shout and bang on the gate with their farm tools until they were allowed back inside.

The Japanese prisoners at Cowra were

much different. Sgt. Maj. Ryo Kanazawa, 26, was typical. A veteran of six years of service with the Japanese Army, Kanazawa had fought in China and had been wounded there. He still carried one bullet in his hip and another in his thigh.

Twice Kanazawa had been singled out for heroic feats. He had been awarded the Order of the Rising Sun and the Order of the Sacred Treasure. Kanazawa followed the tradition of Bushido.

Kanazawa had been on a troop transport that had been bombed and sunk in the Coral Sea off the coast of New Guinea. He drifted in a crowded lifeboat for six days before reaching the New Guinea coast. He and several companions headed into the jungle. They had no food or water. Kanazawa fell ill with malaria. He struggled on for several days before falling in his tracks. When an Australian patrol found him, Kanazawa was unconscious.

Kanazawa would not give his right name when questioned by the Australians. He invented the name Akira and started using it. The shame of being taken captive was so great that Kanazawa could not bear to have his family find out that he had fallen into enemy hands. Akira was the name that went into the prison records.

At Cowra, Kanazawa became a camp

leader. He was older than most of his comrades. He was — at five feet nine — taller than most of them. He had a perfect military record. He was tough and experienced.

Kanazawa and the other Japanese prisoners showed their distress at being held captive in several different ways. They complained about the food and refused to answer when roll call was taken. Although most of the officers had a working knowledge of the English language, when given an order in English, they would look around in a puzzled manner as if they had never heard the language spoken before.

Isamu Naka, a Japanese lieutenant, was one of the hardest prisoners to handle. He frequently took a shower when roll call was being taken. During camp inspections, Lieutenant Naka often went to bed.

The Japanese prisoners were treated well by the Australians. They were given plenty of good food to eat. Many gained weight, in fact. They lived in comfortable, well-heated buildings. They did not have to work. They were even given a weekly ration of cigarettes.

While Japanese accepted what they were given, they looked upon these privileges as a sign of weakness on the part of the Australians. The better the treatment they received, the more the Japanese sneered and felt contempt for their captors.

The Japanese thought about escaping constantly. Finally they agreed on a mass escape; they would all break out at once.

Some would storm the barbed wire fencing that surrounded the camp, throwing blankets, coats, or heavy padding over the strands before climbing over them. Other prisoners would attack the camp's guard posts and main gates.

Some of the guard posts were equipped with machine guns. The Japanese had no guns. They realized that in charging the machine gun posts many of them would be committing suicide.

"We will die as warriors," said one of the prisoners. "I have been thinking each day of some way to kill myself because I can't bear the thought of being a prisoner any longer.

"Now we can die in combat. We can bring some honor to our families after all."

By the early days of August 1944, B Compound at Cowra, one of the pie-shaped sections where the Japanese soldiers were held, was bursting at the seams. It held 1,104 prisoners, about twice as many as it had been built to hold.

To reduce the crowding, the Australians planned to transfer about half the prisoners in B Compound to another prison camp about two hundred miles farther west, Those to be transferred were all enlisted men of the rank of corporal and below. They were to leave in two well-guarded trainloads on Monday, August 7.

When the Japanese prisoners learned about the transfer, they became enraged, not so much at the idea of the transfer itself, but because the Australians planned to divide the prisoners by rank. In sending the enlisted men to the second camp, they would be separating them from the noncommissioned officers — the NCOs. In the Japanese army, the NCOs were like older brothers to those men of lesser rank, to the privates and corporals. It was unthinkable to separate them.

Sergeant Major Kanazawa spoke to one of the Australian officers about the transfer. "Is it true?" Kanazawa asked. "Do they really intend to separate us according to rank?"

"It's true," said the officer.

"Can't you ask Major Ramsey [the camp commander] to reconsider?"

"I've already asked him once. He told me it's not in his power. The instructions have come from somewhere else. It's his job to carry them out."

Kanazawa was grim. "We don't like

this," he said. "We'll have to do something."

The officer shrugged. "There's nothing you can do," he said, "except get ready to make the change."

Kanazawa, his mind reeling, hurried back to his barracks and sought out several of his friends. "I think we have to do it now," he told them. "If we don't act quickly, it will be too late."

His friends nodded in agreement. It was not a matter for debate.

"We have to realize," Kanazawa said, "that others might not feel as we do. Let's talk to the barracks' leaders as soon as we can, and they'll talk to the men."

After dinner that night, there were meetings in each of the barracks. Some were quiet; others, emotional.

In one of the barracks, Kiyoshi Yamamoto called upon his men to die for the spirit of Bushido. "Our comrades who died in battle are calling to us," he said to his men. "Close your eyes tonight and you will hear them. This is the moment we have waited so long for."

Yoshio Shimoyama, another barracks' leader, echoed what Yamamoto had said. "You're Japanese," said Shimoyama. "You must feel ashamed to be here. Now you have the chance you have waited for. There is no choice. You have to go. Does anybody disagree?"

Nobody did.

Other groups of men had doubts, however. "I don't really feel we should make the break," Seiji Ogi told his men. "But if the whole camp wants to go, I think we should go along with them."

In some barracks, a vote was taken. Slips of paper were passed out. A circle was used to indicate that a prisoner wanted to take part in the break. A cross meant he was against it. Some groups voted by a show of hands.

After the meetings, the leaders met. "What is the verdict?" Kanazawa asked.

Shimoyama was the first to speak. "My men want to go," he said. "They are ready to fight and die."

Other leaders agreed. Those who weren't quite so eager to be included in the mass escape were at least willing to go along with the majority.

"There is no doubt about it — we break!" said Kanazawa after everyone had spoken. "Go back to your barracks," he instructed, "and make sure everyone knows we're moving tonight."

Kanazawa had final instructions. "I want it understood that Australian civilians are not to be harmed in any way," he said. "Soldiers are our targets. They are our enemy. Nobody touches civilians."

Shortly before 2 A.M., Tadao Minami sounded a blast on the bugle. That was the signal. Within seconds, the Japanese were pouring out of their barracks and charging in waves in each of several different directions.

More than a hundred Japanese swept toward a machine gun post beyond the barbed wire fences at the northern end of the camp. The gun was unmanned at the time Minami's bugle sounded. But the two-man Australian gun crew, Pvt. Benjamin Hardy and Pvt. Ralph Jones, acted fast. They threw on overcoats over their flannel pajamas and raced for the gun, just managing to reach it before the Japanese.

Hardy started firing. The Japanese kept coming. Tossing blankets and overcoats over the barbed wire, they surged toward the gun. Some fell dead; others were wounded. But they never stopped attacking.

Suddenly the searchlight above the gun went black. Indeed, the entire camp was plunged into darkness. A ricocheting bullet had cut a vital electric cable.

Hardy, now aided by moonlight, continued firing. But he could not stem the tide of Japanese. Wielding clubs and knives, the screaming mob of Japanese overwhelmed the two Australians, then spun the gun around to point it toward the Australians' guard house.

But the gun jammed. The Japanese tried and tried but they could not get it to fire again.

Meanwhile, another stream of prisoners headed for a strip of unguarded barbed wire. They also flung blankets and overcoats over the wire to protect themselves from the barbs. Some of the Japanese wore baseball gloves on one hand. The gloves enabled them to grasp the strands with one hand and climb the fence. Or they raised the bottommost strands and crawled under them.

A sentry armed with a rifle fired into the prisoners as they spilled over and through the fence. But he ran out of ammunition before he could slow them down. They poured out of the camps by the dozens.

Other groups of prisoners surged out onto Broadway and charged the heavy gate at the road's northern end, which was guarded by a machine gun atop a sentry post. The gun crew was ready as the prisoners approached. As the gun chattered, Japanese fell dead or dived into ditches beside the road. Only a handful reached the gate. None got past it.

At the other end of Broadway, the Japanese did not do any better. The machine gun there jammed at first. But once it started firing, scores of Japanese fell dead or were forced to take shelter in roadside ditches.

At the beginning, the local population was terrified at the thought of hundreds of enemy soldiers wandering around the countryside.

Some small towns in the area became armed camps, with civilians as well as military men prowling the streets with rifles and pistols. Other groups scoured the rugged countryside on horseback.

In homes where there was no man available to protect women and children, soldiers were sent to guard them.

Even teenage boys, some as young as thirteen or fourteen, were called upon for patrol duty.

The fears of the people proved groundless, however. So well did the Japanese follow their orders not to harm civilians that not a single act of violence occurred against nonsoldiers.

Seiji Ogi, after spending the night and most of the next day under the bridge, was hungry and thirsty. He had been joined by three other prisoners, all of them younger than he was.

"Let's see if we can find a farmhouse and break into it," said Ogi. "But remember, we don't attack civilians."

They crossed several low hills and came upon a small farmhouse. The three youngsters were ready to give themselves up. But Ogi wasn't sure what he wanted to do. "You go," he said to the others.

Ogi watched from a distance as the three young men approached the house, knocked at the front door, and were admitted.

They were in the home of Walter Weir, a cattle farmer. Mr. Weir was away from the house at the time, but his wife handled the situation calmly.

When the prisoners showed her by gestures that they were hungry, Mrs. Weir prepared hot tea and biscuits for them. While the water for the tea was being heated, she telephoned the prison camp and asked that someone come and pick up the the prisoners.

The three Japanese ate and drank in silence and then bowed their thank yous. When the guards from the prison arrived, they went quietly.

Ogi watched as his friends were taken away. He wandered about for a while, unsure of which direction to go. Suddenly he heard a voice behind him say, "Hold it, mate."

Ogi turned to face a farmer with a raised shotgun in his hands. There were two teenage boys at his side.

The farmer signaled Ogi to move ahead. Before long, they came to a farmhouse. The farmer called the prison camp. Then he asked Ogi: "You want coffee? Bread?"

"Both," Ogi answered.

Although the coffee was boiling hot, Ogi gulped it down. Then he grinned at the farmer's wife and thanked her in both English and Japanese. After the army truck and guards arrived, Ogi bowed and shook hands with the couple.

Willie Bates, 13, was bird-watching when he spotted a Japanese soldier in a tree. He talked to the man until Australian soldiers arrived. Even then, the prisoner refused to climb down from this hiding place until an Australian guard fired shots into the branches above his head.

On his way back to camp, the same prisoner jumped from the truck and tried to escape. He was shot in the leg and recaptured.

Alfred Chambers, 15, served milk to two Japanese he came upon near the farmhouse where he lived. Alf got a reward. Before they were taken away by the Australians, one of the Japanese removed his belt and presented it to Alf as a souvenir. The man insisted, however, on being given a short length of rope to use in its place.

Other Japanese surrendered singly or in groups. Within nine days, all had been rounded up.

Sergeant Major Kanazawa surrendered without a struggle. He was captured with several other prisoners on a road north of the camp.

"I am responsible for the whole thing," Kanazawa told the guards who seized him. "I must be executed."

After being put on trial for his role in the break, Kanazawa was sentenced to fifteen months of hard labor.

For years, the Australian government sought to keep the uprising a secret. News reports about the mass escape referred to it as "The Cowra Incident." But no details were given, and there was no mention of the more than two hundred deaths that had occurred.

Authorities were afraid that if the Japanese learned what had happened at Cowra, they would seek revenge against the Australian captives who were being held in Japanese prison camps.

Today, the remains of the Japanese prisers who died in the uprising lie in neat rows of graves in a well-cared for, tree-shaded cemetery outside of Cowra. Each grave has a cement marker that bears the name of the deceased.

In 1964, the Australian government decided that the cemetery should serve as a memorial to all Japanese killed in the service of their nation during World War II. The bodies of other Japanese servicemen who had died elsewhere in Australia during the war were brought to Cowra for reburial.

The citizens of Cowra have built a Japanese garden and cultural center and established a sister-city relationship with Inazawa, Japan.

So strong are the ties between Cowra and Japan, that few Japanese tourists would think of going to Australia without visiting Cowra. Some of the visitors have been survivors of the Cowra breakout, or relatives of survivors. Members of the royal family have also visited Cowra.

Because of this activity, it is not likely that "The Cowra Incident" or the men who rushed from their barracks to certain death that August night in 1944 will ever be forgotten.

The Great Escape

During World War II, hundreds of prisoners, most of them using only their bare hands or the crudest of tools, tunneled their way to freedom. Some of the most spectacular escapes of the war, in fact, were made by tunnelers.

Tunneling was hard work. But often there was no other choice. Cell keys could not be copied. Locks could not be picked. Guards could not be bribed. Going over the wall was impossible. Going under it was the last resort.

In Europe, where thousands of Allied prisoners were held, the Germans developed many techniques to catch tunnelers at work. Guards kept alert for the tinest disturbance in the earth's surface. They kept on the lookout for any trace of sand that might suddenly appear. Either of these could be the tip-off that a tunnel was being dug somewhere.

The Germans planted microphones in the ground to pick up sounds of digging or the voices of the tunnel workers.

Once the Germans found out a tunnel was being excavated, they usually allowed the prisoners to keep digging until they were on the brink of freedom. At the last moment, the guards would stand poised over the tunnel's exit point. As the prisoners came forth one by one, they would be arrested and placed in solitary confinement.

One of the most exciting stories to come out of World War II tells of a tunnel escape that involved many hundreds of men who worked for more than a year. The story is told in full by Paul Brickhill in *The Great Escape*, which has been called the best escape book of World War II.

The story begins in 1942, just as the Allied air offensive, which was to play a major part in the defeat of Germany and Italy, was beginning to get serious. With American and British bombers making daily raids over Europe, a good many planes were shot down. Many of the crew members died, but some parachuted to safety and were captured.

As the number of prisoners grew, the Germans opened special camps to hold them. One such camp was built at Sagan, a town of about 25,000, some one hundred miles south and west of Berlin near Germany's border with Poland. The Germans called the camp Stalag Luft III. The first two hundred prisoners arrived there in the spring of 1942.

The prisoners' new home was called the North Compound. It was a perfect square, almost one quarter of a mile on each side.

Within the North Compound were fifteen wooden barracks arranged in three rows, five barracks to a row. At one end of the compound was an open area the prisoners used for recreation. It was also where they lined up for roll call.

Surrounding the compound were two barbed wire fences. The innermost fence was charged with electricity. When touched, it triggered an alarm, and guards came running.

The second fence was around twenty feet beyond the first one. It was about nine feet high and strung with some twenty strands of barbed wire. In between the strands coiled barbed wire had been strung. There was so much barbed wire, in fact, that one could scarcely see through the fence.

Watchtowers had been erected every few hundred feet within the outermost fence. Atop each tower stood an armed sentry.

At night, other sentries patrolled the fences. And still another guard prowled within the compound with an attack dog on a leash. When ordered to do so, the dog would go for a man's throat.

The land beyond the fences in every direction was thickly wooded. The trees, mostly tall pine, grew so close together that from a distance they gave the appearance of a great wooden wall.

Within hours after the first British and American prisoners arrived at the North Compound, they began laying plans for a tunnel escape. An escape committee was formed. It was headed by thirty-year-old Roger Bushell, a big man with blue eyes and broad shoulders. A squadron leader with the Royal Air Force, Bushell was captured after his Spitfire had crash-landed in German-occupied France.

Bushell and the escape committee made plans to dig not one tunnel but three of them, and dig them all at the same time. Hundreds of men would be involved. The Germans, the prisoners figured, might find one of the tunnels or even two of them. But they would never find all three.

Bushell realized that were the Germans

to hear anyone mention the word "tunnel," they would get suspicious immediately. So Bushell named the three tunnels Tom, Dick, and Harry. The prisoners were told to always refer to the tunnels by their nicknames. The word "tunnel" itself was never to be used.

Each of the tunnels was to be thirty feet deep. Each was to have its own construction crew.

The first step was to make an accurate map of the camp and find out as much as they could about the area just outside the fence. Then they could decide where to place the tunnels and how long each would be.

Once the tunnels had been mapped out, the next step was to decide upon a starting point for each. This was no easy matter. The Germans had built the barracks so that the floor of each was two feet above the ground. This enabled the guards to crawl underneath each building to inspect the soil to determine whether any digging had been taking place.

But the defense the Germans had devised was not perfect. The washrooms in each barracks and the area of each barracks where the stove stood required a foundation of brick and concrete. The tunnelers focused on these areas in fixing the starting point for each tunnel.

For the tunnel named Dick, a clever trapdoor was built in the washroom of Block 122. In the middle of the washroom floor, there was a concrete drain that was about eighteen inches square, just big enough for a man to fit through. The drain was covered with an iron grating.

One of the prisoners, a specialist in building trapdoors for tunnels, chipped away one wall of the concrete drain until he reached soft earth underneath which was just right for tunneling.

Using cement that had been left behind by German workmen in the compound, he cast a new concrete slab to fit into the opening he had created in the side of the drain. When the tunnelers were ready to dig, the slab was removed. When no one was digging, the slab was slipped into place, the cracks filled with soap and sand, and the iron grate put back on top. It was practically impossible to tell that there was a tunnel entrance in the side of the drain.

The trapdoor for Harry was constructed in a similar fashion beneath the stove in Block 104. Tom began in a dark corner of the concrete floor of the washroom in Block ·123.

Shovels for diggers were made from pieces of metal taken from old stoves. When the dirt was hard-packed, the tunnelers hacked away at it with chisels made by filing down table knives.

Tunnelers had to work naked or wear long underwear, carrying their clothing in bundles. Tunnel dirt on anyone's clothing would be a tip-off to the Germans that digging was going on.

Tunneling was tough work. The tunnel was just wide enough for a man's shoulders. Digger No. 1 would lie in front, scraping away dirt from in front of his face, and shoving it back to Digger No. 2 behind him.

It was hot. The men never stopped sweating. The air was foul.

After the tunnel was thirty or so feet in length, small four-wheeled carts were built to transport the sand from where the diggers were working to the other end.

A long rope was attached to each end of the cart. When the cart was filled with sand, Digger No. 2 tugged on the rope. That was a signal to a man at the tunnel entrance, who hauled the cart toward him. As soon as the cart was emptied, Digger No. 2 hauled it back.

Light came from primitive torches. For fuel, the prisoners saved animal fat from table scraps. They also used margarine. A piece of pajama cord served as a wick.

The tunnel walls and ceilings had to be supported with wooden boards. Otherwise, they would cave in. The prisoners used their bedboards for tunnel supports. Carpenters cut them to fit.

As the tunnels kept getting longer, the men doing the digging called for more and more boards. In the final stages of tunneling, every bed in camp was short at least three boards. Mattresses sagged through the spaces, but the prisoners got used to it.

Crude pumps were built to empty the foul air and bring fresh air in. Each pump was made of a cloth bag over a ribbed wooden frame. It worked on the same idea as an accordion, folding in and out. When pushed in, the pump forced air out of the tunnel; when pulled out, it sucked air in.

There was also a simple alarm system. It consisted of a tin can with pebbles in the bottom that had a long string attached and was suspended from the tunnel ceiling. When a guard approached, a worker near the tunnel entrance tugged the string, rattling the stones. All work ceased until the guard left.

During the first few feet of digging, the tunnelers removed gray dirt. But underneath there was bright yellow sand, which caused a problem. Anytime the guards spotted yellow sand, they knew immediately that there was a tunnel being dug somewhere. Searches were instantly launched to find it.

With three tunnels being dug, there would be tons of yellow sand to get rid of. But how? Hiding all that sand was something like trying to hide a bowl of Jell-O in a thimble.

The prisoners agreed that they would never be able to tunnel their way out until they found a way to camouflage the sand.

"Everyone should dig gardens outside their huts," one prisoner suggested. "Then the yellow sand will turn up naturally. The Germans won't be suspicious of that."

"That's a good idea," said another, "as long as we don't let the level of the gardens get any higher."

The first man had an answer to that. "What we can do is save the gray topsoil from the garden and replace it with yellow tunnel sand in the gardens. Then we'll mix the gray sand with the rest of the tunnel sand and spread it around the compound."

Bushell's brow wrinkled. "But how are you going to spread the gray-and-yellow sand mixture around without being spotted?" he asked.

Peter Fanshawe, a British pilot, had been thinking about that. "With trouser bags," he said, and from his pocket he pulled what looked like a long, white cloth sack. The sack was something that Fanshawe had made from a leg he had cut off a pair of long underwear. To the top of the sack, he had tied a long length of string.

Fanshawe explained that when you looped the string around your neck under your shirt, you could hang the bag down the inside of one of your trouser legs.

The trouser bag had a pin stuck in the bottom. A string was tied to the pin. The string, Fanshawe explained, led up inside the trousers to a pants pocket.

It worked like this: You filled the trouser bag with yellow sand and wandered around the compound until you came to a good spot for spreading it. You pulled the string in your pocket. Out came the pin. The sand came trickling out the bottom of your trouser leg.

"Great! We'll try it immediately," said Bushell.

Dozens of prisoners made themselves trouser bags. The long underwear they used came from packages that the Red Cross had sent. Long underwear was one of the few things the prisoners had plenty of.

The tunnel shaft for Tom was getting deeper and deeper. Two of the tunnelers would scrape the yellow sand into metal cans. The cans would then be passed up to

Tom Minskewitz, an American prisoner, who was stationed in the washroom where the tunnel began.

Minskewitz had blankets spread out around the hole so none of the sand would be spilled on the floor. Prisoners would enter the washroom with their trouser bags, hand them to Minskewitz, who would fill them, and then wander out into the yard.

Sometimes the spreaders would work in groups. Jerry Sage, another American prisoner, had organized about forty men who practiced marching and precise military movements as a form of recreation. Bushell spoke to Sage and got him to agree to put a dozen or so men wearing trouser bags in the middle of the formation.

As the men marched, the yellow sand was shuffled onto the parade grounds. Gray sand from the gardens was sprinkled over any spot where too much yellow sand had collected.

Volleyball games were also used to get rid of the sand. Many of the prisoners who stood at the sidelines cheering and clapping wore trouser bags.

One day one of the men assigned to get rid of yellow sand got a little careless. He was one of the prisoners watching a volleyball game, and he pulled the pin out of his trouser bag when he was standing behind the crowd instead of in the center of it. The yellow sand never got mixed in with the gray topsoil.

One of the guards spotted the sand before the prisoners had time to cover it up. He reported his find to Sgt. Peter Glemnitz, who was in charge of camp security.

The next morning, dozens of guards with shovels entered the compound. They dug up all the gardens. In several of them, they found more yellow sand than should have been there. Now the Germans were really suspicious.

"Glemnitz knows there's a tunnel," Bushell told a meeting of the committee. "There won't be any peace until he finds it. Glemnitz is going to start watching the compound like a hawk."

"Have you seen the guards in the watchtowers?" someone asked. "Every one of them has got his binoculars up. They're watching us all the time."

"They're probably keeping a count of the number of people that go in an out of every barracks," said Bushell. "We have to cut back on the amount of people-traffic in and out of Block 123."

"What about spreading the sand?" another man asked. "It's going to be risky."

"We'll put some of it in the gardens

where they've already found sand," Bushell said. "I know the Germans. They won't think of looking there."

The next day, the Germans tried another tactic. At about eleven o'clock in the morning, three heavy trucks were brought into camp. They were driven back and forth across the prison yard, mostly along the sides of the barracks. The Germans were hoping that the trucks would collapse any tunnel with their weight. But Tom, Dick, and Harry, thirty feet down, were safe.

Hardly a day passed without one or more of the barracks being thoroughly searched by the Germans. They scoured Block 123 one morning and came out with a few nails and some wire — all they were able to find in almost four hours of searching.

Another day the prisoners in Block 107 found two German guards hiding in the roof. They had climbed up during roll call and had their ears glued to the ceiling. They hoped to hear the prisoners discussing escape plans. But the guards were discovered before any of the prisoners revealed anything.

Because of the increased watchfulness on the part of the Germans, digging was slowed to almost a halt. Sometimes the tunnels advanced by only a few feet a day.

Then the Germans found more freshly spread yellow sand in the garden of Block 119. Glemnitz was furious. He ordered everyone out of Blocks 106, 107, and 123 and had them searched. But nothing of importance was found.

Glemnitz wasn't going to give up. That morning a formation of about a hundred German troops marched into the compound. They were followed by a truck carrying shovels and picks.

About half the soldiers grabbed tools and started digging. Before long, they had dug a long trench about four feet deep. Two of the soldiers then took steel rods about five feet long and began hammering them through the bottom of the trench. They were hoping to hit the roof boards of a tunnel. Bushell, standing with his arms folded, watched silently.

When the soldiers had sunk a rod as far as it could go, and it failed to strike anything, they would pull it up and try again about a foot away. Once they did hit something about a foot down. Half a dozen soldiers were put to work digging at the spot. They finally reached what the rod had struck. It was a rock. Bushell and the other Americans who were watching couldn't stop laughing.

At nightfall, after a day of digging without finding any trace of Tom, Dick, or Harry, the Germans gave up. The soldiers filled in the trenches and left.

"They must be pretty sure we've got something going," Roger Bushell told a gathering in his room that night. "If they get any more evidence, they'll go crazy. We can't afford another mistake. Glemnitz mustn't find any more sand."

"Why not," said Fanshawe, "put sand down Dick?"

That was the perfect solution. In the days that followed, the prisoners carried sand from Tom into the washroom of Block 122. There it was passed along to the far end of Dick, and it was dumped.

The wooden boards that supported the walls and roof of Dick were removed and used in Tom. Work went ahead briskly. Some days Tom advanced by as much as ten feet. Eventually, Tom reached a point under the edge of the woods.

Then one day the prisoners saw a sight that made their hearts sink. German soldiers were hard at work in the wooded area beyond the western fence, cutting down trees and clearing away the brush. Within a few days, they had moved back the edge of the woods by a hundred feet or so.

The tunnelers were bitter. Thanks to their hard work, Tom was now just over two hundred feet in length, and they were approaching the finish line. But all of a sudden they had another hundred feet to go.

Nevertheless, Roger and the others agreed on one thing — they would go on digging.

When Tom was 260 feet long, Bushell decided it had gone far enough. It was still about forty feet from the wooded area but it was 140 feet beyond the outermost fence. Just as important, it was well past the light thrown by the searchlights atop the sentry boxes. Bushell and other members of the committee agreed it would be safe to break out at that point. They figured it would take about four days to dig from the tunnel level up to the surface.

Then disaster struck. One day Glemnitz ordered a surprise search of Blocks 104 and 105. At the last minute, he switched plans and sent searchers into Block 123. Bushell and several other men watched from Block 122 as the Germans looked for traces of tunneling.

One of the guards was ordered to take an iron rod and tap every square inch of floor in the washroom of Block 123. If one of the taps resulted in a hollow sound, it might tip off the existence of a tunnel.

Suddenly the tip of the rock stuck in the

concrete. The guard got down on his hands and knees to investigate. When he saw the outline of a trapdoor, he let out a shout.

Within minutes, Glemnitz had arrived upon the scene and stood by as a guard with a sledgehammer smashed the trapdoor. Another guard was sent down the ladder. It took him half an hour to crawl to the end of Tom and back again.

Glemnitz was beaming. He ordered the tunnel to be destroyed with explosives.

Tom was no more. A wave of sadness swept over the prisoners.

Bushell called a meeting. "We started the project with three tunnels, knowing that we might lose one or two of them," Bushell reminded the men. "We've still got two, and the Germans probably think we don't have any.

"We're going ahead," Bushell promised. "I don't think they'll stop us this time."

Bushell ordered Dick to be used as a storage area for clothing and other supplies and equipment the men would need after they escaped. The men doing the digging concentrated on Harry.

Winter and freezing temperatures arrived. During December, the camp was covered with a foot of snow. It was no time for escaping. Tunnel operations were shut down.

Early the next year, when digging began again, everything went smoothly. There were days the men advanced the tunnel by eleven or twelve feet. One day they carefully measured the tunnel from one end to the other. Harry stretched 348 feet.

The tunnelers estimated that it was 335 feet from where the tunnel began to the edge of the woods beyond the fence. In other words, they had gone as far as they had to go. The next step was to dig up — and out.

The tunnelers scooped out dirt until they came to the roots of trees. They knew then they were near the surface. The No. 1 Digger tested how far they had to go with a metal rod, sticking it through the top of the shaft. When he had pushed the rod only about six inches, he felt no more resistance.

Only six inches to go! The tunnelers stopped digging and roofed over the top of the shaft. Then they went back to announce the good news — Harry was finished!

Now the prisoners made final preparations for the escape. They wanted the break to take place on a moonless night. They also wanted good weather.

Bushell and the others checked a calendar. The 23rd, 24th, and 25th were moonless nights. They decided that March 24th would be the date.

Bushell and the committee figured out

that as many at 220 men might be able to get through the tunnel on the night of the break. Some 600 men had taken part in the project.

Bushell and the others picked ninety men from the 600. They were the men who had worked the hardest on the project. They would go first.

The remaining 610 names were put into a hat and 130 names drawn out. These men were to go in the order in which their names had been drawn.

They were told to get ready. Each was given a fake name and forged identification papers. They were also provided with civilian clothes, food, maps, and money from other prisoner committees.

March 24th dawned sunny and mild. Bushell and the committee met in Roger's room. It was a very short meeting. All agreed, there could be no turning back. "Tonight's the night!" Roger announced. "Let's get going!"

After dark, the men who were to break out began to trickle into Block 104. One by one, they climbed down the ladder and crawled into the tunnel. Eventually the first seventeen men were in position within the tunnel, waiting for it to be opened at the end.

Johnny Bull climbed to the top of the

ladder, removed the roof boards, and scraped away the last few inches of sand. As his shovel broke through, he felt the cool night air rush in. He widened the hole so he could get his head through. What he saw paralyzed him. The tunnelers had slipped up. Harry wasn't long enough. Instead of ending up inside the woods, the exit was about ten feet short of the woods. Just as bad, maybe worse, a sentry post was only about forty feet away.

When the news that the tunnel was short was reported back to Bushell, he shook his head sadly. But he realized if they stopped now and delayed the break, they would have to postpone it for another full month, until another moonless night. "We can't put it off," Bushell said firmly. "We've got to go tonight."

One by one, the men began crawling out of the hole. Each would pause for a moment to make certain he had not been spotted by the guard, then crawled off toward the woods. Inside the trees, each got to his feet and walked away.

And so it went through the night. Ten men got free, then twenty, thirty, forty, and fifty.

Bob McBride was to be the eightieth man out of the hole. He had mounted the ladder and started climbing when he heard a rifle shot and then a whistle's shriek. When McBride looked toward the tunnel opening, he saw the barrel of a rifle pointing at his head. The guards had discovered what was going on. The show was over.

When the Germans learned that scores of British and American prisoners were on the loose, they launched a massive search. Many thousands of troops were involved. They stopped and searched vehicles. They checked homes and farmhouses and trains. They patrolled the roads.

One by one, the men who had escaped were rounded up. Three got free and made their way to England.

The next year, on June 6, 1944, British, American, and Canadian forces crossed the English Channel to launch an invasion of France. Meanwhile, the Russian armies rolled toward Germany from the east.

On May 9, 1945, Germany surrendered. After five years, eight months, and seven days, World War II in Europe was over.

With the war's end, stories of incredible escapes began to be heard. But for tension and thrills, for ingenuity and persistence, few stories equaled that of the British and American air force officers of the North Compound of Stalag Luft III.